500
FLOWER & ANIMAL
CROSS STITCH DESIGNS

500
FLOWER & ANIMAL
CROSS STITCH DESIGNS

JULIE HASLER

Text by
VALERIE JANITCH

David & Charles

(Above) *Unicorn picture*
An ingenious and easily constructed plastic frame
surrounds a majestic unicorn. Worked with two
strands of cotton (floss) on 14-count Aida, the
unicorn can be found on Chart 95

(Page 1) *Framed flower*
A stylised flower set in an oval brass frame. Just
press the embroidery, then mount it in the frame and
seal it with the special locking device. The flower
design is on Chart 102

(Opposite) *Brooches and pill box designs*
These delightful designs are worked with two
strands of embroidery cotton (floss) on 18-count
Aida fabric. The owl's head can be found on Chart
22, the design set into the lid of the little pot is on
Chart 4, and the flower on the tiny pill box is from
Chart 24

(Page 2) *Elephant nursery picture*
Elephants on their way to a party, taking their own
balloons! Worked on easy to count 14-count white
Aida fabric with two strands of cotton (floss), the
design is outlined and detailed with a single strand of
black. This design is on Charts 111 and 112

(Page 2) *Circus train nursery picture*
Stitched on 14-count white Aida fabric with two
strands of cotton (floss) and outlined with a single
strand, this lovely nursery picture can be found on
Charts 113 and 114

A DAVID & CHARLES BOOK

First published in the UK in 1996

Designs & charts Copyright © Julie Hasler 1996
Text Copyright © Valerie Janitch 1996
Photography and layout Copyright © David &
Charles 1996

Julie Hasler has asserted her right to be identified
as author of this work in accordance with the
Copyright, Designs and Patents Act, 1988.

A catalogue record for this book is available from the
British Library.

ISBN 0 7153 0288 4

Photography by Di Lewis
Typeset by Ace Filmsetting Ltd, Frome
and printed in Italy by Nuovo Istituto Italiano
d'Arti Grafiche – Bergamo
for David & Charles
Brunel House   Newton Abbot   Devon

CONTENTS

INTRODUCTION

ARLY examples of cross-stitch designs are usually geometric patterns used as borders, but later the fascination for pictorial samplers developed, and with it the representation of familiar objects. By far the most popular – as is the case in all embroidery – were the flora and fauna which people saw in the world around them. Sometimes the subjects were the actual flowers, fruit, birds and animals that they knew in the countryside; on other occasions they were exotic extravagances created purely for their decorative appeal.

Flower and animal designs, both natural and stylised, are no less popular today – the demand seems to be insatiable. So here is a vast collection of motifs from which to choose when you are designing your own embroidery. There are plants and flowers, leaves and trees, birds and butterflies, fish and shells, and other exotica – even a unicorn! Whatever you are seeking, you will find subjects for every taste and to suit every purpose.

Large, small and tiny motifs, borders and frames – whatever you require, you are sure to find all the ideas and inspiration you need in the following charts. And alongside the designs there are lots of imaginative suggestions for suitable applications, with full details of how to complete each project. First, a general count-down to cross stitch is provided for those who are not already expert in this quick, easy and fascinating field of embroidery.

(Opposite) *Floral and animal bookmarks*
These ready-to-embroider bookmarks in white and cream 18-count Aida fabric need no making up when you've finished stitching. The floral designs are on Chart 12, the squirrels on Chart 51, and the pigs taken from the alphabet on Charts 126–128

Puffin picture
A delightful study shown in a circular gilded frame, with a watch top hanger. Protected by either acetate or glass, the embroidery is easily secured inside. The cross stitch is worked with two threads over 14-count cream Aida. The puffin design is on Chart 94

1

PLANNING AND PREPARATION

ROSS stitchers generally approach the subject in one of two ways: either they want to make something, and they know what they want to make; or they want to make *something* . . . but their primary concern is to do some cross stitch, and they don't really know *what* to make. More often than not, the latter is the case. So this book sets out to give you not only an overwhelming choice of charted designs for the cross-stitch piece itself, but a whole host of ideas for things to do with your work when it is finished. This ensures that you won't be left holding a charming little piece of embroidery – with no purposeful application.

The first thing to do, then, if you haven't already got something definite in mind, is to decide on a project. The second thing to do is to choose a suitable design. And the third is to plan the design to fit the project. Then you will be able to start your embroidery happy in the knowledge that, whilst you are enjoying the work itself, there is also an exciting end-product ahead.

Having said that, if you have never cross stitched before, it is wise to start with a test piece – just to get the hang of things. Choose the simplest possible design: not more than two colours, and quite small, so that you don't waste much time on your practice piece before you get going on the real thing. The following chapters tell you all you need to know to start, and explain the technique of cross stitch itself. When you have mastered that, you will be anxious to start on something specific, so there is no harm in thinking about it at this stage!

Horses card

A pair of high-spirited young horses – quick and easy to embroider in a single colour, with only a touch of contrast for their glittering black eyes. Worked with two strands of cotton (floss) over 14-count Aida fabric, this is an ideal card for a man – or, of course, anyone who is mad about horses! This design, and more, is on Chart 96

Flying bats card

This is the perfect card for Hallowe'en! The dramatic colour scheme creates an eye-catching card, perfectly suitable for a message of any kind. Or it would solve that other perennial problem: finding a suitable birthday card for a man. Worked with two strands, for greatest coverage and impact, on 18-count Aida fabric, the design can be found on Chart 78

Goose greetings card

An exquisite card that the recipient is certain to treasure for a long time to come. The very simplicity of the design gives this card its charm, and the wild rose border around the oval frame adds a final touch of enchantment. White embroidery on a white 14-count Aida ground is outlined in silver-grey. The goose is on Chart 102, and there are more on Chart 101

Fishes card

Twin fishes – an imaginative card for a Pisces' birthday, perhaps? Suitable for most occasions, the subject is depicted in shades of blue and green on a white ground, suggesting a clear blue sea. This card is a good example to show the importance of choosing a setting that enhances the subject: the pale aqua-tinted mount sets the watery theme off to perfection. Worked on 14-count Aida, the fishes can be found on Chart 94

Those who are already hooked should waste no time before going through the photographs to decide what to make. There is a wide variety of delightful items – as you can see – and lots more practical applications appear on the charts themselves, where there are ideas for specific designs, as well as suggestions for different colourways and alternative presentations. Your experience will help you visualise these and assess whether they are to your taste.

DECIDING WHAT TO MAKE

Begin with something simple – like a greetings card. There is an enormous range of card mounts available, both plain and decorated. It will help your choice if you have already decided on your embroidery, but if you have not, it doesn't matter: the card you buy will dictate the design. You will also need a pad of graph paper.

You will find a full description of the types of fabric available in the following chapter. But the most popular among cross-stitch enthusiasts is called *14-count Aida*. Aida is the name of the fabric (describing the weave that forms the blocks over which one stitches): 14-count means that there are fourteen stitches to the inch (2.5cm), cross stitch – or 'evenweave' – fabrics are always counted to the imperial inch. So it is recommended that you start with a piece of 14-count Aida, which you can buy as a small piece, 11in (28cm) square. You do not need to buy this yet; wait until you have worked out your design, then you can choose your fabric and embroidery cottons (floss) at the same time. The important thing is to know that you will be working on a 14-count fabric.

MEASURING UP THE PROJECT

The first thing to do is to measure the area of the 'window' or aperture on your card, in inches. Now draw the shape out on the graph paper allowing fourteen squares in each direction for each square inch. So if your window measured

$4 \times 2\frac{1}{2}$in (10×6.5cm) you would need 56×35 squares marked out on your graph paper:

$$4 \times 14 = 56 \quad \text{and} \quad 2\frac{1}{2} \times 14 = 35$$

Now you know the exact size and shape of the area that you have available for your design, so search through the book for a motif that will fit comfortably into this area (allowing a little space all round it). All you have to do is to compare the number of squares occupied by the charted design, with the number of squares in the outline marked on your graph paper. So if, for instance, a design is thirty-six squares in depth and twenty-seven squares wide, it will fit nicely within the window of your card.

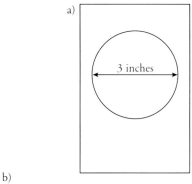

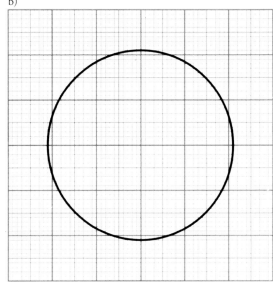

Fig 1 a) A card with a 3in (7.5cm) diameter window
b) The circle drawn up on graph paper for 14-count embroidery, $3 \times 14 = 42$ squares

This is the basic principle of working out the size of a design to fit your chosen area, and you can use it in any situation. In time, as you explore the other counts, you will discover how to make a design fit if it is too large, by using a higher count fabric. For instance, a 16-count fabric will give you sixteen stitches to the inch, making the design smaller and an 18-count will give you eighteen stitches to the inch – making it smaller still. In each case, you would draw the outline shape on your graph paper with sixteen or eighteen squares to the inch respectively.

VISUALISING THE DESIGN

When you have found just the right design for your 14-count fabric, you can, if you like, visualise exactly how it will look by copying it from the chart onto your graph paper. Place a ruler over the design and mark the centre with a tiny line – in both directions – so that you have a small cross (+) in the middle of the design. Mark the centre of the outlined area on your graph paper in the same way. Then copy the charted design onto the graph paper, matching the

Towel borders
Towels take on a whole new identity when you appliqué on an embroidered Aida band. These two were perfectly plain and ordinary, until they changed their identity with designs from Charts 74 (the ducklings) and 93 (the starfish and shells). Worked with two strands of embroidery cotton (floss), they pick up the colours of the scalloped edges

centre points. It is not necessary to do this, but if it is your first attempt, it will give you a very good indication of how your chosen design will look on the card, and how well it will fit.

Now is the moment to go out and buy your fabric and threads. The fabric can be white, cream or coloured and there is a wide range of shades available. There is also a vast selection of stranded embroidery cottons (floss) to choose from – prepare to be overwhelmed! For your first piece of work, you will find it easier to follow the colours shown on the charted design. But for future embroideries, you can change these around as much as you please, substituting a completely different colour scheme for the one

shown. Doing this, and choosing the cottons and background fabric, are all part of the fun of cross stitch. Enjoy it!

METRIC AND IMPERIAL MEASUREMENTS

Working in cross stitch is a little more complicated for those who are accustomed to using metric measurements. Embroidery fabrics, as already mentioned, tend to be calculated to the inch, so remember to work in imperial measure. US readers will, of course, have no problem with this.

However, in other instances where both metric and imperial measurements are stated, you will notice that the conversions are not absolutely accurate. Instead, the designs are calculated individually to give you the convenience of working with straightforward amounts.

Jar lacies

What could be more appropriate for a farmhouse kitchen, or old-fashioned tea-table, than a cross-stitched 'jar lacy' to cover the pots of jam, jelly, honey, marmalade or preserves? The delicate embroidery is worked with two strands of cotton (floss) over 18-count Aida fabric, which is surrounded by heavy lace. The apple and cherries are on Chart 17, the swallows on Chart 73, and the flower on Chart 80. 18-count Aida can be embroidered with either one or two strands of cotton (floss); although one strand is easier, and perfectly adequate, if you want the body of the motif to be quite dense – as in this case – it is worth using two strands. Pull the threads quite taut – especially the lower half of the stitch – without actually pulling them tight. This will avoid unsightly loops or a bumpy overall effect when the work is finished. These ready-made covers are easy to launder, and the only finishing touch you have to add is half a yard (50cm) of a pretty colour-matched ribbon, threaded through holes in the lace and tied in a bow The ribbons are by Offray

2

EQUIPMENT AND MATERIALS

EEDLES and scissors are the two most important pieces of equipment in your workbasket. Cross stitch is worked with a small blunt tapestry needle (size 24 or 26). Have several of these needles, and take good care of them by keeping them in a special pincushion or a needlecase. When you need to use pins, they should be fine and sharp.

Two pairs of scissors are necessary. You will need a large pair to cut the fabric and a small pair of embroidery scissors to cut your threads. Both should be sharp and well aligned. Sharpen them regularly – an electric knife and scissors grinder does the job quickly and very efficiently. A separate pair of scissors which you can reserve to cut paper is an advantage. Occasionally, you will need to cut up paper for charts, and this tends to blunt scissors very quickly.

Although cross stitch may be worked in the hand, to ensure a perfectly smooth and even finish the fabric should be stretched taut. You can achieve this easily with an embroidery hoop. Choose a 4in (10cm), 5in (12.5cm) or 6in (15cm) diameter plastic or wooden hoop, with a screw-type tension adjuster. Larger pieces of embroidery should be worked on a frame. Ask your local needlecraft shop to show you a selection, and advise you.

CHART-MAKING EQUIPMENT

As mentioned in Chapter One, a pad of graph paper is essential. This does not need to be an expensive one from a special shop; you can get it from any ordinary stationers. It can be imperial or metric measure, it doesn't matter, as long as each inch or two centimetres is divided into 10×10 tiny squares (like the charts in this book). There is usually also a faint sub-division into 5×5 tiny squares. The bolder lines are a great help, both when you are copying out charts, and when you are working the design. When you copy out a design, always follow the heavy lines on the original chart in the book, as this prevents mistakes.

Have a well-sharpened fairly soft pencil (HB or B) and a soft eraser (for the inevitable odd mistake!), a ruler and something with which to colour the charts. For colouring you can use watercolour paints, coloured pencils or felt-tip pens. All are perfectly good, though you have to take care that watercolours do not run into each other. On balance, pencils or felt-tip pens are probably quicker, but you can get a more accurate representation of colour by mixing paints.

When you are making up a charted design, for a sampler for instance, you will want to stick small pieces of graph paper onto a larger background sheet. Use a dry stick adhesive like UHU Stic, an all-purpose clear adhesive like UHU, or a special transparent mending tape like 3M Magic Scotch tape which has a matt surface so that you can write on it.

FABRICS TO USE

Cross stitch can only be worked over an 'evenweave' fabric. That is to say one where

there is exactly the same number of threads to the inch in each direction, so that when you work one cross stitch, the width and depth will be exactly the same. And, when you work a square block of ten cross stitches, the width and depth will again be exactly the same. If the fabric was not exactly evenly woven, it may not be apparent in one stitch – but it would begin to become very obvious on a larger block, which, when stitching was finished, would not be square.

There are various types of evenweave fabrics that you can use. The most common is the one we have already encountered: *Aida*. The threads in this are quite fine, and woven in blocks. Each cross stitch is worked over a block of threads. If there are fourteen blocks to the inch, this is called 14-count and will give you fourteen stitches to the inch. Aida bands are also available: in several widths, from 1in (2.5cm) to 4in (10cm), they have plain or coloured, scalloped or woven, borders. These make a quick and easy decoration when appliquéed to towels, garments and soft furnishings. They are ideal for curtain tie-backs, and make an attractive band for a straw hat, too. Simply cut the required length of band, and then repeat your embroidered design

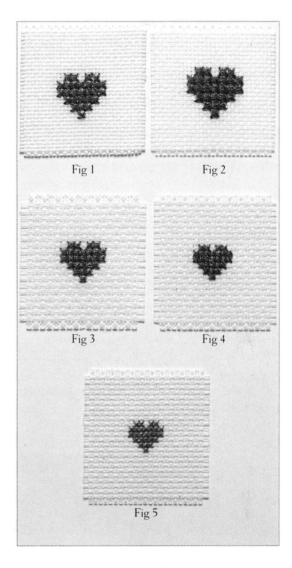

Fig 1   Fig 2

Fig 3   Fig 4

Fig 5

(Opposite left) *Window pictures*
Two exquisite embroideries make up a pair of windows, showing how small, extremely simple designs can be built up to form an artistic arrangement – emphasised by the fine work involved. The designs are worked on 22-count white Hardanger fabric with a single strand of embroidery cotton (floss), beautifully complemented by the deep rose mounts and gold embossed rose frames. The designs are on Charts 35 and 36

(Opposite right) *Sampler pictures*
A pair of beautifully worked pictures embroidered on 22-count white Hardanger fabric with a single strand of cotton (floss). The related colour schemes echo the vibrant golds and burning oranges of the setting sun, and are beautifully complemented by deep maroon mounts surrounded by dark wood frames. Note the unusual shape of the mounts, which set off each picture to even greater advantage. The designs are from Charts 37 and 41

Fig 1   25-count evenweave fabric (Lugana), giving 12½ stitches to the inch (2.5cm), worked with two strands of embroidery cotton (floss)

Fig 2   22-count Hardanger fabric, giving eleven stitches to the inch (2.5cm), worked with three strands of embroidery cotton (floss)

Fig 3   14-count Aida fabric, giving fourteen stitches to the inch (2.5cm), worked with two strands of embroidery cotton (floss)

Fig 4   16-count Aida fabric, giving sixteen stitches to the inch (2.5cm), worked with two strands of embroidery cotton (floss)

Fig 5   18-count Aida fabric, giving eighteen stitches to the inch (2.5cm), worked with one single strand of embroidery cotton (floss)

along it. The bands are described in detail on Chart 18, and illustrated in the photograph on page 11.

Also available is evenweave *linen*, or its cotton equivalent, like Linda. Here the weave is more conventional, and the threads are single. In this case, each stitch is worked over *two* threads in each direction. So this time a 28-count fabric will give you fourteen stitches to the inch.

Finally there is *Hardanger*, which is between Aida and linen. It is woven with pairs of finer threads, and a cross stitch should usually cover two pairs of threads in each direction. However, for very fine work, the stitch may be worked over a single pair of threads in each direction.

All these fabrics are available in a variety of thread counts, and a very good range of colours. They also come in various widths, but you can buy smaller pieces in special packs. Remember, the more crosses to the inch, the smaller your stitches will be. And the fewer crosses to the inch, the larger they will be. As already mentioned, fourteen stitches per inch is a good average count to begin with, it is the count that the majority of people feel most comfortable with, and also the one that offers the greatest choice of colours.

You will also find *waste canvas* very useful. This allows you to embroider on fabrics where cross stitch would not normally be possible because there are no evenweave threads to follow. Simply tack (baste) the plain white canvas over the area you wish to embroider – work the cross stitch over the canvas and through the fabric – then pull away the threads of canvas by dampening the work thoroughly to dissolve the glue which holds them together. A full description of waste canvas is to be found on Chart 85.

Animal fridge magnets
Cross stitch can be practical – and amusing – as well as pretty. And you cannot get much more practical than these amusing fridge magnets. Worked on 14-count Aida fabric, the completed embroidery is simply cut to size and slid between the two plastic surfaces of the magnet. The turtle is on Chart 52, the penguin on Chart 56, the rabbit on Chart 60, the mouse on Chart 61, the whale on Chart 68, and the seahorse on Chart 93

THREADS TO USE

You will find an interesting variety of threads at your needlecraft shop, but all the examples in this book are worked with stranded embroidery cotton (floss), which is generally considered the most satisfactory for this type of cross stitch. DMC six-strand embroidery cottons (floss) come in a truly magnificent range of colours, which means that they offer breath-taking shading effects.

In use, the strands are separated. The number that you use depends on the fabric – the smaller your crosses, the fewer strands you will need. Two or three strands are the most usual: use two strands for twelve or more stitches to the inch (2.5cm) and three strands for eleven or less stitches to the inch (2.5cm). For very fine work, use only one strand.

Gift tag selection

A tiny, simple motif suddenly comes alive when it is made into a smart little gift tag – giving your message as much importance as the gift itself. The strawberry, bunny and duckling are all embroidered on 18-count Aida, but the dirty paw print makes its mark on 14-count fabric! The duck can be found on Chart 4, the strawberry on Chart 61, the rabbit on Chart 64, and the paw print on Chart 67

Key-ring fob designs

Such an easy way to show you care for someone – a tiny cross-stitch motif sealed in the fob of a key ring makes a practical and very personal gift, but takes little more than minutes to do. These three examples are all embroidered with two strands of cotton (floss) on 14-count Aida. The ladybird is on Chart 3, the flower on Chart 12, and the heart on Chart 62

3

BEGINNING THE EMBROIDERY

EFORE you begin the embroidery of your chosen design, prevent the cut edges of your fabric fraying by either whip-stitching or machine-stitching all round. Alternatively, turn under and tack a small hem. The latter method has the advantage of also preventing your embroidery cottons (floss) snagging and snarling against the cut edges.

WHERE TO START

First find the centre points of the chart and your fabric. If you begin stitching from the centre, you can be sure that your design will be correctly positioned. If you want your design to be placed off-centre on the fabric you will need to find the centre of the design itself, but you can still follow the method given below.

To find the centre point of the chart, place a ruler horizontally across the middle, and measure and mark the centre of the design itself with a tiny line. Then place your ruler vertically over the design and do the same thing – making a small cross (+). The centre of the cross is the centre of your chart (Fig 1). Alternatively, of course, you can count the squares in each direction and divide the number in half to find the centre.

To find the centre point of the fabric, fold it in half and crease the fold. Then fold it in the other direction and crease the fold again. Make a line of tacking (basting) stitches in contrasting cotton along each fold, following the woven threads.

Cat and mouse initial card
Just one of the attractive alphabets in the book supplies the initials for this personalised card worked with two strands of cotton (floss) on 14-count Aida. An amusing theme, carried right through from A to Z, shows a mouse tantalising a cat. The alphabet is on Charts 118–120

Floral initial card
Nothing could be more satisfying than to receive a card with one's own initial embroidered on it. The harebells are repeated in the design below the aperture of this very special card. It is worked on 14-count Aida. The initial comes from the alphabet on Charts 123–125

Name finger-plates
These are very easy to embroider on 14-count Aida fabric. Jane's name is taken from the alphabet on Charts 123–125, and Neil's from the alphabet on Charts 126–128

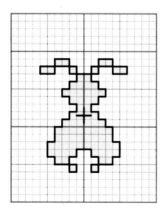

Fig 1   Marking the centre of a charted design

The point where the two lines cross is the equivalent to the cross (+) on your chart.

Sometimes it is not practical to start stitching at the centre of the design. When this is the case, count the number of squares or stitches from the centre of the chart to the point where you want to begin, then count the same number of blocks or double threads on your fabric.

GETTING READY

Cut off the required amount of cotton (floss); you will find 18–20in (45–50cm) is a comfortable length to work with. One at a time, gently draw out the number of strands that you require. If you are working on a 14-count fabric, you will need two strands. Then put the individual strands together again. Remember always to do this, as it ensures a neat, full stitch which covers the block properly.

Thread the needle, but *never* make a knot! Knots create bumps at the back of your work, and spoil the smooth surface of the finished embroidery. Instead, you must weave the tail ends of the thread – at the beginning and end of each bit of embroidery – through the back of existing stitches (see figs 4 and 9 opposite).

Place the remaining strands of cotton (floss) in a thread holder. This may be purchased, or you can make your own from two strips of stiff card between which you have fixed small curtain rings with double-sided tape (Fig 2). Mark the shade number above each ring (in pencil, so that you can erase it to use the holder again for another set of threads).

If you are using an embroidery hoop allow approximately 2½in (6cm) more fabric than the size of the outer ring of the hoop all round. To place the fabric in the hoop, rest the area to be embroidered over the inner ring and carefully push the outer ring down over it. Pull the fabric gently and evenly, making sure that it is drum taut in the hoop, and that the weave is straight, tightening the screw adjuster as you do so.

When working, you will find it best to have the screw in the 'ten o'clock' position, as this will prevent the thread becoming tangled with the

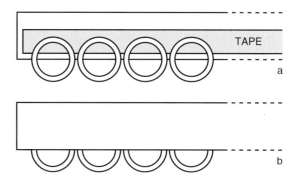

Fig 2   Make your own thread tidy from curtain rings taped between two strips of card

screw as you stitch. If you are left-handed, have the screw in the 'one o'clock' position. As you work, re-tighten the fabric every so often, to keep it taut.

STARTING TO CROSS STITCH

All the designs are worked with full cross stitches, although occasionally a half cross is used (forming a triangle, instead of a square). Sometimes a design is outlined in backstitch, which gives it added emphasis. Back-stitching can also be used most effectively to pick out detail. The only other stitch which appears is a French knot, which is sometimes used for eyes, etc.

As previously explained, the cross is usually worked over a complete block of an Aida fabric; over two threads in each direction of an evenweave linen or cotton; and over two pairs of threads of a Hardanger fabric. If your design incorporates half crosses, you will find it easier to stitch on a fabric where you work over pairs of threads, rather than solid blocks.

To begin the first stitch, bring the needle up from the wrong side, through a hole in the fabric at the left-hand corner of the stitch (Fig 3); leave a short length underneath and weave it neatly through the backs of the first few stitches, once you have made them (Fig 4).

To work an individual or isolated cross stitch bring the needle diagonally up across the pairs of threads or block that you want to cover, and take it down through the hole at the right-hand corner (Fig 3). This is the first half of your stitch. The needle is now at the back of the fabric. Take the thread straight down and bring your needle up through the bottom right-hand hole (Fig 5): then take the thread diagonally across and up to the remaining corner at the top left, pushing the needle down through it (Fig 5). Your cross stitch is now complete.

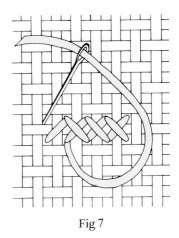

Fig 7

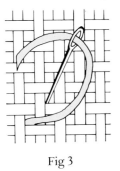

Fig 3

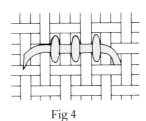

Fig 4

Fig 5

Fig 8

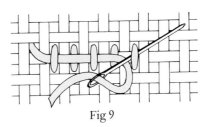

Fig 9

If you have a horizontal row of stitches in the same colour, work the first half of all the stitches across the line (Fig 6): then return and complete the crosses (Fig 7). Work vertical rows of stitches in the same way (Fig 8).

Finish off your thread on the wrong side, by running your needle under the backs of four or more stitches (Fig 9).

NOTE: To simplify the working diagrams as much as possible, each vertical and horizontal thread on Figs 3–10 represents a *block* of threads on an Aida fabric; a *pair* of threads on an evenweave linen or cotton; or *two pairs* of threads on a Hardanger fabric.

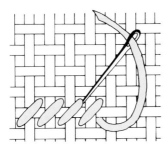

Fig 6   Diagrams showing actual method of cross stitch and backstitch

FRENCH KNOTS

These stitches are ideal for adding small features to designs, such as animal eyes and noses. To make a French knot bring the needle up from the wrong side and wind the thread around it twice. Push the needle down through the fabric one thread, or part of a block, away from the starting point to finish (Fig 10).

Fig 10

OUTLINING AND DETAILING IN BACKSTITCH

Some of the designs are outlined with backstitch to give them greater clarity or emphasis. Backstitch is also used to pick out fine details. Always work the backstitch after all the cross-stitch embroidery is finished, using one strand less than you used for the cross stitch.

Backstitch is worked from hole to hole, following the same blocks as the cross stitches, and can be stitched in vertical, horizontal or diagonal lines, as Fig 11. Take care not to pull the stitches too tight, or the contrast of colour will be lost. Begin, and finish off, as for cross stitch.

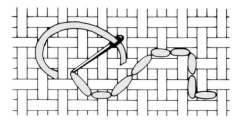

Fig 11

KEEPING COUNT

If you have difficulty in counting when working on 14-count Aida, there is an ingenious version of the fabric that has a coloured thread woven into it every ten squares. When you embroider on this type of Aida, you can align the marker threads to the heavy lines on the chart you are following. This makes counting child's-play, and it is almost impossible to go wrong. When the work is completed, all you have to do is to pull out the grey marker threads.

Here are two more tips to help you keep your place on the chart. The first is to place a ruler on top, or slide a hair grip down the side, when working lines of embroidery, to indicate where you are. The second is to copy out the design, then either draw a line through, or colour in, each area of cross stitch as you embroider it.

SOME HINTS AND TIPS

It is important to keep your tension even – if it is not, the fabric will be pulled out of shape. If you are worried about this happening, use a hoop, as described earlier in this chapter. Work each stitch by pushing your needle straight up through the fabric, and then straight down again, keeping the fabric smooth and taut. There should be no slack, but don't pull the thread too tight – draw it through so that it lies snug and flat.

Do not carry threads across the back of an open expanse of fabric. If you are working separate areas of the same colour, finish off and then begin again. Loose threads, especially dark colours, will be visible from the right side of your work when the project is finished.

If the thread becomes twisted while you are working, drop the needle and let it hang down freely. It will untwist itself. Don't continue working with twisted thread, as it will appear thinner, and won't cover the fabric satisfactorily.

Never leave the needle in the design area of your work between embroidery sessions. Not only might it distort the fabric, but no matter how good the needle, it could rust if left for any length of time, and leave a permanent mark.

Bull's head pen stand and paper clip container
This polished wood pen stand would look wonderful with a piece of your needlework set into the lid. Worked with two strands of cotton (floss) on 14-count Aida fabric, the bull's head is on Chart 63

Paperweight designs
These paperweights, made from heavy glass, are simplicity itself to put together. Worked on 14-count Aida with two strands of cotton (floss), the floral design is on Chart 23, the flamingo on Chart 53 and the ram's head on Chart 63

Cockerel cabinet
Made in dark wood, this charming small collector's cabinet is an obvious place to display a piece of your needlework. The chart for the strutting cockerel is shown on Chart 47

4

MAKING UP THE FINISHED WORK

HE first thing you must do when you have completed your embroidery is to press it. You will be surprised how professional your work looks after it has been carefully pressed!

Prepare a smooth, softly padded surface – or fold a thick towel – and place the fabric right-side down on it. Then cover the back with a thin, thoroughly damp cloth and press evenly and gently. Leave the embroidery until it is cool and dry.

BACKING PICTURES AND SAMPLERS

Whether or not you plan to frame a picture or sampler, it will need to be mounted on a firm backing. You can buy a self-adhesive board which is specially made for this purpose, or you can use an ordinary acid-free stiff mounting board or foam board (available from artists' suppliers).

Cut a piece of board exactly the size of the finished design, having allowed at least 2in (5cm) surplus fabric all round the design. You can allow less – 1¼in (3cm) – on smaller pieces, but for larger items, it is wise to allow a greater amount of excess fabric round the edge.

There are two ways to fix the overlapping fabric round the edges of the board: you can either oversew it to the edges, or lace it across the back. In each case, place the embroidery face up on the board, positioned so that the edges of the design are exactly level with the edges of the board. To do this, mark all round the edge of the design with a tacking (basting) thread, then pin the fabric carefully to the edge of the board, matching the centres on each side before working outwards to the four corners with your pins (Fig 1). Then mitre the corners as shown in Fig 2 (see page 26).

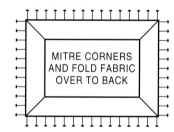

MITRE CORNERS AND FOLD FABRIC OVER TO BACK

Fig 1   Embroidery stretched over mounting board and pinned to the edge

Butterfly miniature
An exquisite embroidered miniature, the butterfly is worked with two threads on 18-count Aida, and set in a particularly lovely little glass-fronted watch top frame. The butterfly design is on Chart 53

Butterfly trinket boxes
The entrancing butterflies are all embroidered on fine 18-count Aida fabric, and set in the lids of a set of ivory porcelain boxes, which look superb wherever you put them – from dressing table to coffee table. They are available individually, in various shapes and sizes, and in a range of colours. The butterflies are from Charts 80, 82 and 83

To hold the fabric in place, either oversew neatly all round the edge (Fig 3) or use strong linen thread to lace together with long stitches the two opposite edges of the surplus fabric, first the top and bottom (Fig 4), and then the two

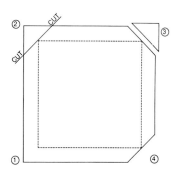

Fig 2　The four stages of mitring a corner

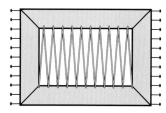

Fig 3　Oversewing the fabric to the edge of the board

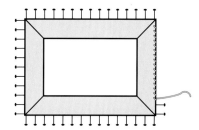

Fig 4　Lacing the top and bottom edges together at the back. Next lace the sides together

sides in the same way, across the first set of lacing stitches. Seal the corners with a smear of clear adhesive, such as UHU, to prevent them fraying.

For very small pieces, you can use double-sided tape to hold the surplus fabric down at the back. Finish off the cut edges neatly by taping over them with a transparent mending tape.

If the picture or sampler is not to be framed,

finish off the back neatly by cutting a piece of cartridge weight paper, or felt, slightly smaller than the finished project. Then fix it over the back with clear adhesive or double-sided tape.

CUSHIONS AND PILLOWS

Although you can make your own inner pads from plain cotton-type fabric and a good quality washable filling material, it is usually more convenient to buy them ready-made, in the size and shape that you require.

As already discussed, you will have had the size and shape in mind when you first planned your cushion or pillow, although when deciding those proportions, it is wise to bear in mind the standard sizes available. Most household department stores and soft furnishings suppliers carry a good range.

Make up your cushion or pillow to the same dimensions as the pad, allowing a good half-inch (about 1.5cm) extra for the seams. This seam allowance applies if you whip- or machine-stitched the raw edges of your cross-stitch fabric before you began the embroidery. However, if you turned under and tacked a small hem instead, take out the tacking threads and either trim the edges to the above seam allowance, and then whip- or machine-stitch them; or if you prefer to leave the edges raw, make the seam allowance a little wider.

 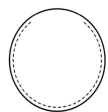

Figs 5 and 6　Joining the front and back of a square or round cushion: leave open as indicated

Cut your backing fabric the same size as the front of the cushion, then join the two pieces, right sides together, all round, leaving the greater part of one side open at the centre, as Fig 5 – or a similar amount on a round cushion (Fig 6).

For a square or rectangular cushion, mitre the corners (see opposite), then turn to the right side and press. Insert your cushion pad and slip-stitch the seam.

For a round cushion, trim and clip the raw edges of the seam – but not too close to the stitching. Then turn the seam allowance at each side of the opening to the wrong side and tack (baste). Turn the cover to the right side and press. Insert your cushion pad and slip-stitch the seam.

A narrow piping cord sewn around the edge gives your cushion a neat and professional appearance.

Wildflower mirror

An arrangement of wildflowers worked on 14-count Aida is the perfect subject with which to decorate this piece, adding nature's colours to accentuate the dark wood. The finished embroidery is mounted behind glass, which is very easy to fit. This attractive design is on Chart 33

Owl candle screen

This adjustable wooden candle screen looks very handsome with a magnificent embroidered owl forming the illustrated panel. The picture area of the screen is 5 × 3½in (13 × 9cm), and the embroidery is worked with two strands of cotton (floss) on 14-count Aida fabric. The owl is on Chart 40

WONDER PRODUCTS

There are three products which offer enormous potential when making up cross-stitch projects. They would make embroiderers of previous centuries green with envy! *Vilene* is a non-woven interlining material that is widely used in dressmaking to interline, reinforce or stiffen garments: you have perhaps used it for this purpose. It comes in a range of weights, from a very fine, almost cobwebby backing for the lightest fabrics, to a thick and heavy stiffening suitable for belts and similar items. All weights are sew-in, but some are iron-on as well – in which case, place the bonded side over the back of the fabric, with a damp cloth on top – and a hot iron will fuse the Vilene to the fabric.

Vilene Bondaweb and *Wundaweb* both look like ordinary Vilene interlining, but they are in fact bonded on *both* sides, allowing one piece of fabric to be fused to another. Bondaweb is paper-backed: when you have cut it to the required size, place the bonded material on the back of one piece of fabric and iron over the paper. When it has cooled, peel the paper away, place the wrong side of the second piece of fabric on top, and iron it into place, using a damp cloth. Wundaweb looks like a tape made from the finest Vilene, and is used to make hems without stitching. The raw edge of the fabric is turned over to the wrong side, the Wundaweb 'tape' is placed between the layers of fabric and the hem is ironed under a damp cloth, when it will become permanently fused together. Full instructions accompany both these products.

CLEANING AND CARING FOR YOUR CROSS STITCH

Cross-stitch embroideries worked on cotton or linen fabrics may be laundered quite safely, if handled with care. For the treatment of work using their stranded embroidery cotton (floss), DMC suggest washing in soapy, warm water. Squeeze without twisting, and hang to dry. Iron the reverse side, using two layers of white linen or cotton. Always wash embroidery separately from your other laundry. Avoid dry cleaning.

Fish and butterfly bell pulls
Two really lovely bell pulls worked on 14-count Aida fabric. Either would make a colourful and eye-catching wall decoration in a hall, living room or bedroom. They would also be perfect for a bathroom, where the deep sea or butterfly theme could be echoed elsewhere. Imagine butterflies here and there on the curtains, or fishes swimming across a guest towel – and that crusty crab on the corner of a towelling bathmat! He would be easy to embroider, using six strands of cotton (floss) over waste canvas. There are butterflies and fish galore throughout the book, and the crab appears on Chart 87

ACKNOWLEDGEMENTS

I would like to thank the following people for their help with this book: Lesley Smith, Dawn-Marie Parmley, Brett Tucker, Simon O'Grady, Sarah Uttridge, Hazel Nutting and Janet Dobney for help and inspiration with design ideas; and Lesley Buckerfield, Jenny Whitlock, Odette Coe, Allison Mortley, Libby Shaw, Joyce Formby, Maureen Hipgrave, Stella Baddeley, Angela Eardley and Lynda Potter for stitching the examples shown in the photographs.

Thanks also to my suppliers: H. W. Peel & Co. Ltd, Norwester House, Fairway Drive, Greenford, Middlesex, UB6 8PW (for graph paper); DMC Creative World Ltd, Pullman Road, Wigston, Leicester, LE8 2DY (for fabrics, threads, Aida bands, coloured flexi-hoops, Keepsake cards and Chelsea Studio cards); and Framecraft Miniatures Ltd, 372–376 Summer Lane, Hockley, Birmingham, B19 3QA (for bell-pulls, collector's cabinet, wooden desk kit, silver-plated jewellery and accessories, paperweights, trinket boxes, glass coasters, fridge magnets, bookmarks, Crafta-cards, jar lacies, miniature brass frames, gift tags, key rings, mirror and candle screen).

When writing to these suppliers, please include a stamped self-addressed envelope.

The card collection
Turning carefully selected designs into greetings cards is a wonderful way to use your work. A simple motif can be transformed by choosing the right card mount to enhance the design. The cards opposite are all worked with two strands of cotton (floss) on 14-count Aida. Choose Aida in different colours for either contrasting or toning with the coloured cards. The traditional sampler motif from Chart 12 is on pure white Aida, and the floral basket from Chart 43 is on pale blue fabric. Another simple flower design, the spring flowers card, features a daffodil from Chart 44. The iris comes from Chart 14

29

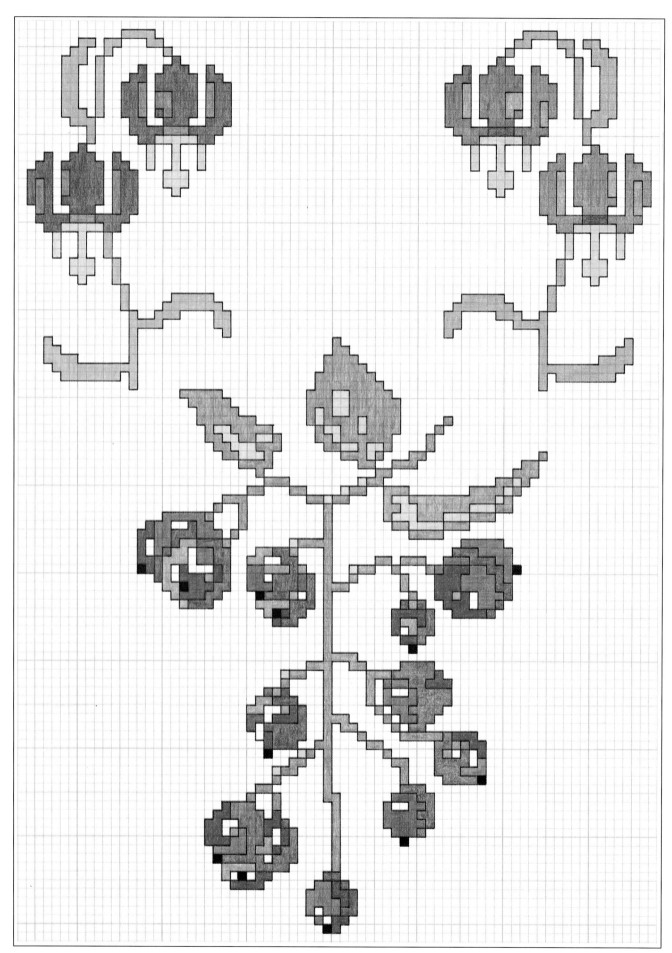

CHART 1 FUCHSIAS AND BERRIES

USING THE DESIGNS

This fuchsia and berry design (Chart 1) would look particularly attractive centred on a cushion cover, perhaps surrounded by a leafy border (see Charts 22, 26, 65 or 115). Make a circular cushion with leaves scattered freely around the central motif: select some from Chart 15.

Divide a square cushion cover into sixteen smaller squares with a narrow border, and embroider a flower in the centre of each, alternating the colours. Instructions for making a cushion are in Chapter 4.

Small floral borders, like the ones on Chart 2, can be used on tablecloths, tray cloths, napkins, place mats, curtains (drapes), towels, or even edging the shelves on an old-fashioned kitchen dresser. They are also ideal for samplers and needlework accessories. You could make a pincushion and matching needlecase, decorating them with one or more of these designs. Such small gifts don't take long to make and are always appreciated.

Making a Book Needlecase
Cut two pieces of stiff card for the front and back of the needlecase. Place them side-by-side on your embroidery fabric, with a narrow gap between for the spine, allow a ½in (1.5cm) surplus all around, and cut out. When the embroidery is complete, place it face down and glue the card lightly to the wrong side. Mitre the corners (see Chapter 4) and turn the fabric over the edge, gluing it to the card. Cut a piece of felt, slightly smaller than the cover, and glue over the back of the card, covering the raw edges of the fabric. Use pinking shears to cut two or three more felt 'pages': place them on top of each other and stitch them down the spine.

CHART 2 PRETTY BORDERS

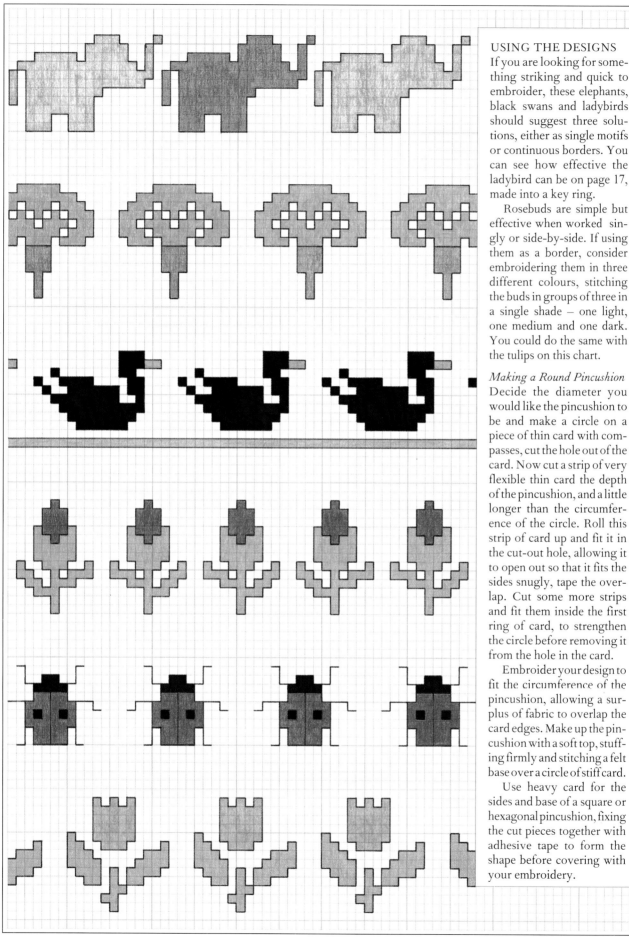

USING THE DESIGNS

If you are looking for something striking and quick to embroider, these elephants, black swans and ladybirds should suggest three solutions, either as single motifs or continuous borders. You can see how effective the ladybird can be on page 17, made into a key ring.

Rosebuds are simple but effective when worked singly or side-by-side. If using them as a border, consider embroidering them in three different colours, stitching the buds in groups of three in a single shade — one light, one medium and one dark. You could do the same with the tulips on this chart.

Making a Round Pincushion
Decide the diameter you would like the pincushion to be and make a circle on a piece of thin card with compasses, cut the hole out of the card. Now cut a strip of very flexible thin card the depth of the pincushion, and a little longer than the circumference of the circle. Roll this strip of card up and fit it in the cut-out hole, allowing it to open out so that it fits the sides snugly, tape the overlap. Cut some more strips and fit them inside the first ring of card, to strengthen the circle before removing it from the hole in the card.

Embroider your design to fit the circumference of the pincushion, allowing a surplus of fabric to overlap the card edges. Make up the pincushion with a soft top, stuffing firmly and stitching a felt base over a circle of stiff card.

Use heavy card for the sides and base of a square or hexagonal pincushion, fixing the cut pieces together with adhesive tape to form the shape before covering with your embroidery.

CHART 3 EASY BORDERS

CHART 4 MORE EASY BORDERS

CHART 5 BORDERS AND FLOWERS

USING THE DESIGNS

The four cornered border designs on this page are ideal for table linens and would look beautiful on place mats, worked in the colours depicted, or in the colours of your choice. Dark shades in particular are very practical for table mats and the blue and white design would look stunning on a navy blue ground. The most favoured embroidery fabric is 14-count Aida, which offers twenty-two colours, although there is a wide range available in all the popular counts.

Making a Place Mat

When embroidering a border design plan it on graph paper beforehand. Decide the size of the mat, and the fabric you wish to use. If, for instance, you choose 14-count Aida, you will need fourteen squares of graph paper in each direction for each inch (2.5cm) of the mat (your paper design will be larger than the finished mat). Draw out the design, following the chart carefully, planning where the border begins and ends and how the corners turn. This way you will not go wrong.

Allow for a hem all round – alternatively, draw threads and hemstitch a fringe. If you want a hem but don't want any stitches to show, use a product like Vilene Wundaweb which is ironed on to the fabric.

CHART 6 BORDERS WITH CORNERS

IDEAS AND ALTERNATIVES

The five border designs, above, are all suitable for place mats. Run either of the first two in horizontal lines across the top and bottom of the mat.

Why not make special Christmas place mats, to be brought out year after year? The bell and holly leaf design, perhaps worked vertically down one side, would make a beautiful set of festive mats. The colours shown here are unusual enough to make them interestingly different. Give them a touch of Christmas sparkle by using a holly green ground and embroidering the bells in silver thread with the leaves in pale grey-green.

Chart 8 offers more suggestions for horizontal, vertical or all-round designs suitable for place mats. For example, the toadstools could be embroidered in a single line along the bottom of a mat.

The square orange and sage design would look very sophisticated embroidered in a vertical line down each side of a mat – or even down one side. Consider outlining the inner motif with a single strand of black, which would make the design stand out in a most striking way. Little touches like this often make all the difference to the impact of a design. A parchment coloured background could be used to good effect.

CHART 7 FLOWERS AND BELLS

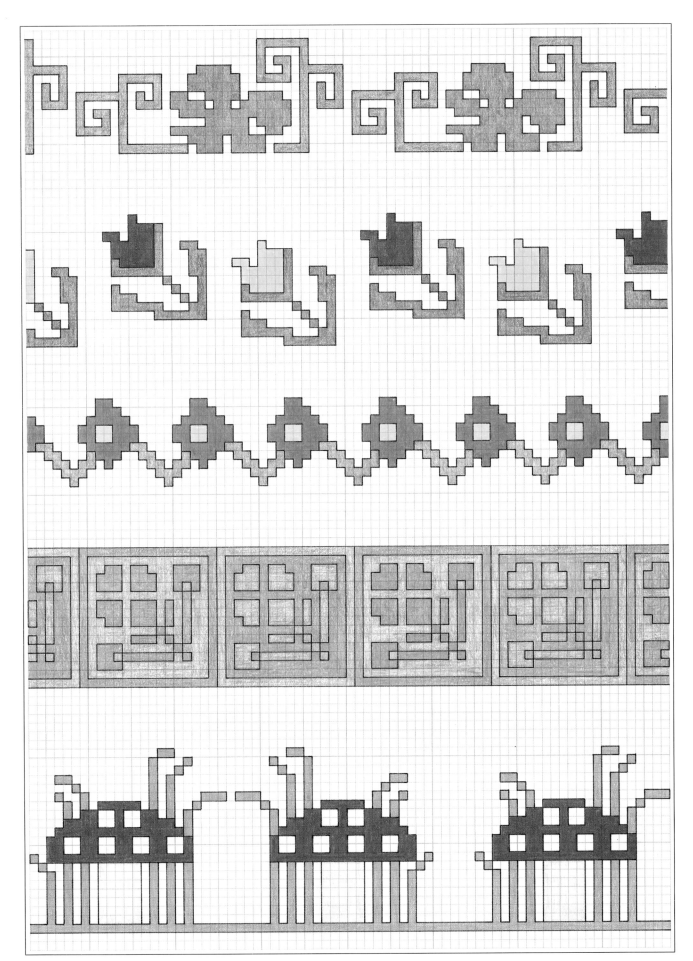

CHART 8 FLOWERS AND TOADSTOOLS

USING THE DESIGNS

Six border designs in even-weave threads that would be especially suitable to embroider on Aida bands. The completed bands could then be sewn onto all kinds of things, such as towels, bibs, napkin rings, curtain (drape) tie-backs and shelf edgings, as well as to heavier items such as thick skirts or slippers which would be difficult to work on, even with waste canvas.

The bands are pretty enough themselves, with either scalloped or woven edges, plain or coloured. Once the embroidery has been finished the decorated band is then just appliquéd into position.

Making a Curtain Tie-Back

If you plan to make curtain (drape) tie-backs, embroider the necessary length of Aida band in the width required, allowing a little extra at each end. Back the embroidery with stiff Vilene to give it body. (The best way to do this is to use either Vilene Wundaweb or Bondaweb to fuse the stiff Vilene into position. Both iron on in the same way, using a damp cloth.) Stitch a small curtain ring at each end of the band, so that you can fix it to a hook screwed into the side of the window. If you are using a band with a coloured edge, choose one which matches either your curtains, or the embroidery.

Attractive tie-backs can transform plain curtains (drapes) making them practical as well as pretty.

You can see examples of Aida bands on page 11, and there are some details of the widths and colours available on Chart 18.

CHART 9 BORDERS FOR BANDS

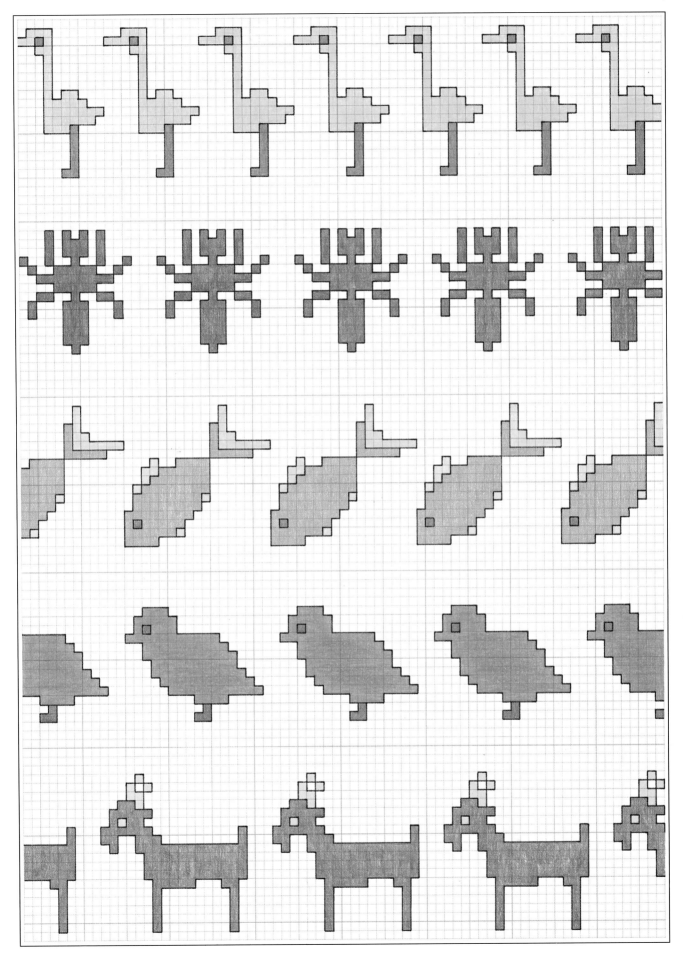

CHART 10 MORE BAND DESIGNS

CHART 11 FLORAL GEOMETRICS

CHART 12 SAMPLER MOTIFS

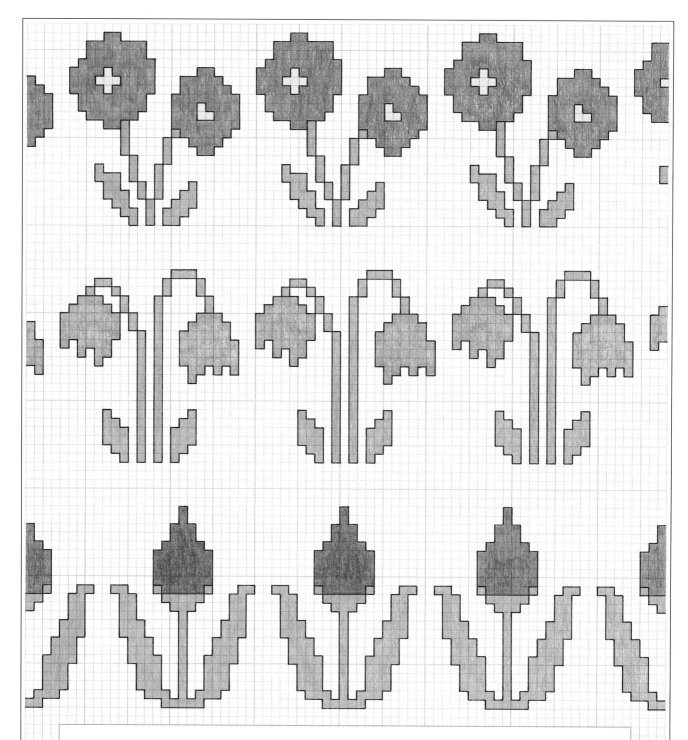

IDEAS AND ALTERNATIVES

Creating a Sampler

The designs on Charts 12 and 13 are ideal for old-fashioned samplers. Select a border, and embroider it in the same colours to give your work a coherent design, then add a selection of other small motifs and, to follow tradition, your initials (see Charts 121, 122, 129 and 130).

The three floral motifs on Chart 13 could also be used individually to decorate small objects, like a pincushion, purse or fridge magnet. Together they make a very pretty square cushion.

Cushion Design 1

Divide the area of your cushion cover equally into thirty-six squares, using lines created by making a cross-stitch over every alternate block. Work a motif in each square, so that you have two of each design in every row – vertically and horizontally, arranging them in a diagonal pattern.

Cushion Design 2

Divide the centre into only nine squares and work one of each motif in every line. Finish with an outer border of leaves near the edge of the cushion (see Chart 65).

CHART 13 HAREBELLS AND ROSEBUDS

CHART 14 OLD-FASHIONED BORDERS

CHART 15 ASSORTED LEAVES

USING THE DESIGNS
Making a Gardener's Notebook
A diary or notebook would look attractive embroidered with the top row motifs, plus the owner's initials. Set the items out in rows across the top and bottom, with the initials in the middle, or dot them around.

Alternatively, arrange four horizontal rows of each single item across the cover, spaced out equally between the top and bottom. Work out any pattern carefully on graph paper before you begin and remember to allow enough surplus fabric for a good-sized overlap.

Making a Gardener's Apron
A gardening apron in heavy cotton poplin makes a practical present. The motifs could form a border along the hem with the initials positioned on the pocket. Use waste canvas for this project, drawing out the threads when the embroidery is finished (details for this method are given on Chart 85).

Make one central pocket, perhaps divided down the centre, in double fabric for strength. Complete the embroidery on a single layer of fabric only, and then make the pocket up afterwards.

CHART 16 JOYOUS GARDENING

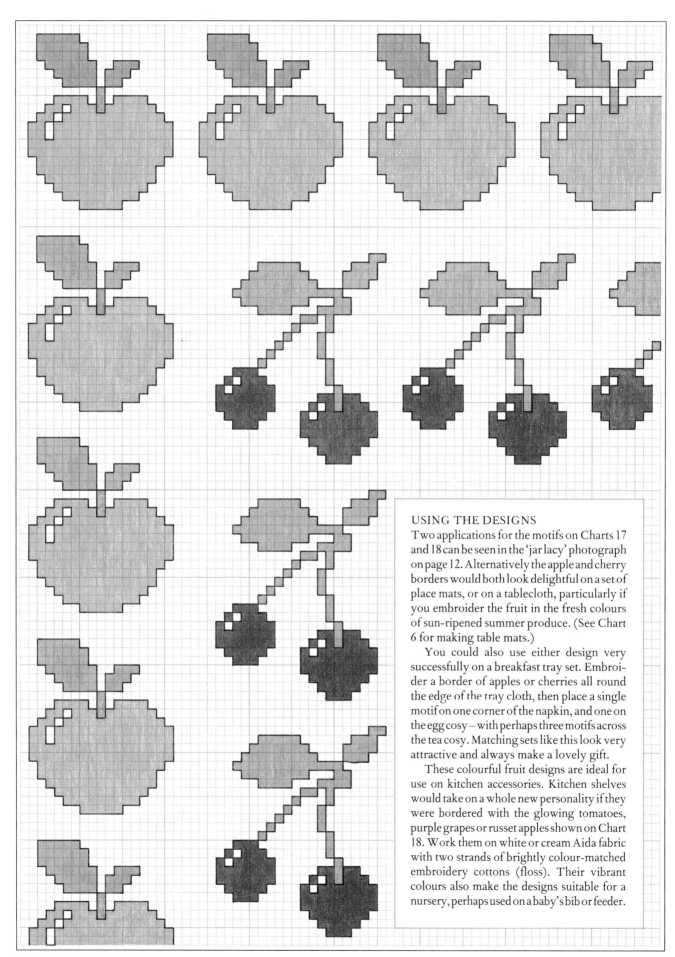

USING THE DESIGNS
Two applications for the motifs on Charts 17 and 18 can be seen in the 'jar lacy' photograph on page 12. Alternatively the apple and cherry borders would both look delightful on a set of place mats, or on a tablecloth, particularly if you embroider the fruit in the fresh colours of sun-ripened summer produce. (See Chart 6 for making table mats.)

You could also use either design very successfully on a breakfast tray set. Embroider a border of apples or cherries all round the edge of the tray cloth, then place a single motif on one corner of the napkin, and one on the egg cosy – with perhaps three motifs across the tea cosy. Matching sets like this look very attractive and always make a lovely gift.

These colourful fruit designs are ideal for use on kitchen accessories. Kitchen shelves would take on a whole new personality if they were bordered with the glowing tomatoes, purple grapes or russet apples shown on Chart 18. Work them on white or cream Aida fabric with two strands of brightly colour-matched embroidery cottons (floss). Their vibrant colours also make the designs suitable for a nursery, perhaps used on a baby's bib or feeder.

CHART 17 APPLES AND CHERRIES

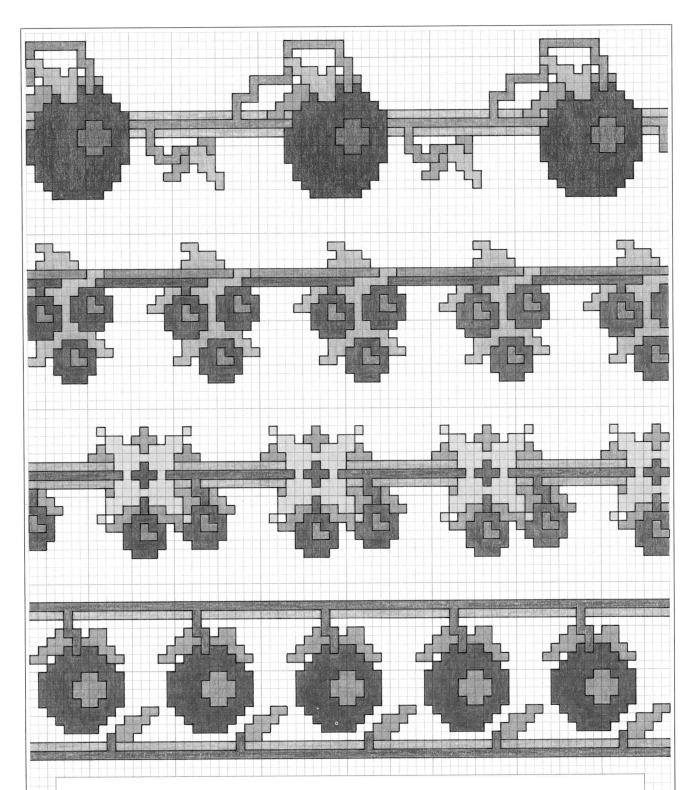

IDEAS AND ALTERNATIVES
Kitchen Shelf Edges

Aida bands with coloured edges are ideal for making kitchen shelf edges. They may have either scalloped or woven edges and come in a variety of widths and colours. The scalloped bands are available in cream and white in three widths: 1in (2.5cm), 2in (5cm) and 4in (10cm). The white bands also come with a choice of coloured edges.

The woven edge bands come in three widths: 2½in (6cm), 3½in (8.5cm) and 4¼in (12cm), in white, and red with a gold edge, which is particularly useful for Christmas decorations.

One very simple festive decoration can be made by embroidering the words 'HAPPY CHRISTMAS' in white or green on a red band, using one of the alphabets shown on Charts 121, 122, 129 or 130. If you would like to add a small motif at each end of your message there is a very suitable border on Chart 7.

CHART 18 ORCHARD HARVEST

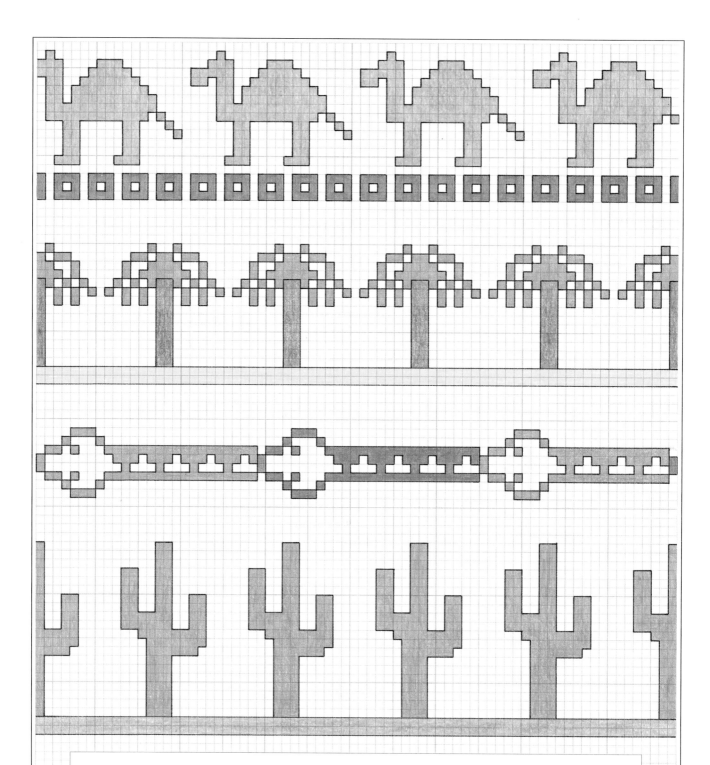

IDEAS AND ALTERNATIVES

There is a strong sense of the desert in this set of subjects, with camels, palm trees, snakes and cacti from which to make your choice; they could form an amusing design for a child's bib or tray cloth.

These motifs are simple to embroider in one solid block of colour; but it is important to outline them with a single strand of embroidery cotton (floss) – either in a very dark brown or black. It is this kind of finishing touch that gives your work character and emphasis.

Likewise, the cacti will be far more effective if you embroider them in, for instance, a mid olive green, outlined with a much darker shade of olive

In the case of the palm trees, embroider the leaves in a bright green, but outline the trunks only. The groundline provides context for this border. It would be a good idea to work a backstitch outline along the *top* edge only, leaving the underneath free of the extra emphasis that the outlining gives.

The simple, but unusual border below the camels is well worth noting as it could come in useful as a narrow frame for a subject or to create a division.

CHART 19 SAND AND HEAT

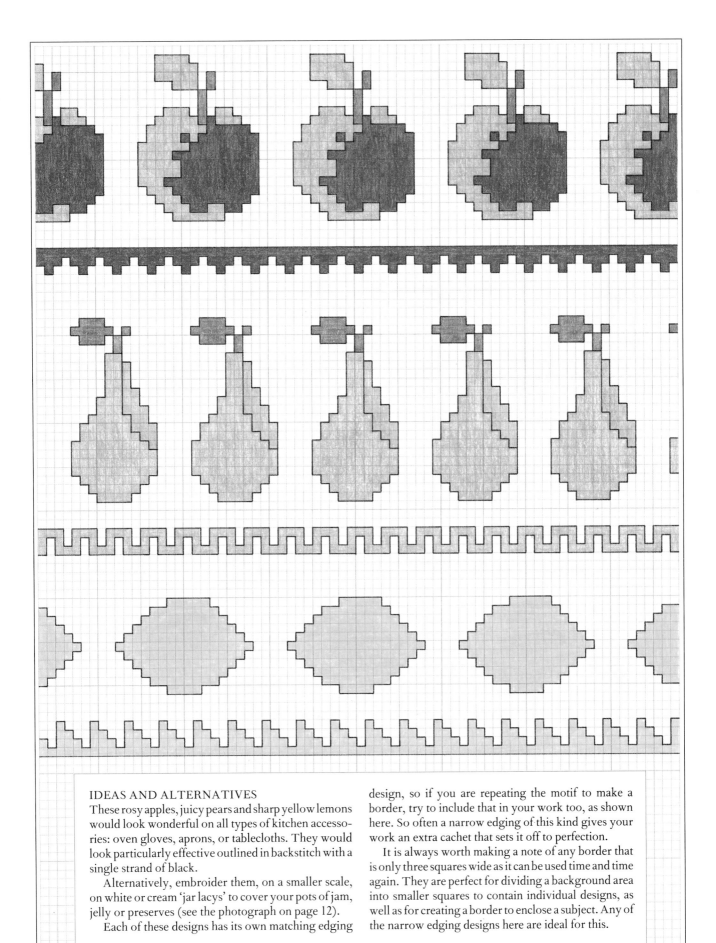

IDEAS AND ALTERNATIVES

These rosy apples, juicy pears and sharp yellow lemons would look wonderful on all types of kitchen accessories: oven gloves, aprons, or tablecloths. They would look particularly effective outlined in backstitch with a single strand of black.

Alternatively, embroider them, on a smaller scale, on white or cream 'jar lacys' to cover your pots of jam, jelly or preserves (see the photograph on page 12).

Each of these designs has its own matching edging design, so if you are repeating the motif to make a border, try to include that in your work too, as shown here. So often a narrow edging of this kind gives your work an extra cachet that sets it off to perfection.

It is always worth making a note of any border that is only three squares wide as it can be used time and time again. They are perfect for dividing a background area into smaller squares to contain individual designs, as well as for creating a border to enclose a subject. Any of the narrow edging designs here are ideal for this.

CHART 20 JUICY FRUITS

CHART 21 GEOMETRIC BORDERS

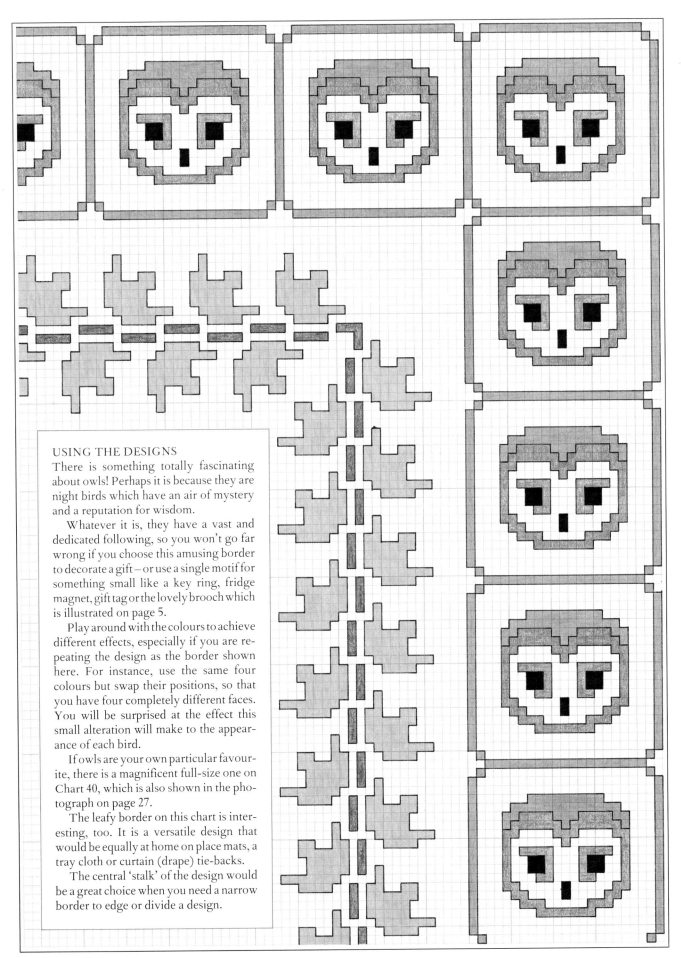

USING THE DESIGNS

There is something totally fascinating about owls! Perhaps it is because they are night birds which have an air of mystery and a reputation for wisdom.

Whatever it is, they have a vast and dedicated following, so you won't go far wrong if you choose this amusing border to decorate a gift – or use a single motif for something small like a key ring, fridge magnet, gift tag or the lovely brooch which is illustrated on page 5.

Play around with the colours to achieve different effects, especially if you are repeating the design as the border shown here. For instance, use the same four colours but swap their positions, so that you have four completely different faces. You will be surprised at the effect this small alteration will make to the appearance of each bird.

If owls are your own particular favourite, there is a magnificent full-size one on Chart 40, which is also shown in the photograph on page 27.

The leafy border on this chart is interesting, too. It is a versatile design that would be equally at home on place mats, a tray cloth or curtain (drape) tie-backs.

The central 'stalk' of the design would be a great choice when you need a narrow border to edge or divide a design.

CHART 22 WISE OWLS

IDEAS AND ALTERNATIVES

Four geometric designs that can prove invaluable when you are really not sure *what* you want but need a fairly quick result. They are ideal for many small items, from key rings and paperweights to greetings cards, needlecases and pincushions.

Whichever one you select, it is wise not to introduce more than two unrelated or contrasting colours into the design. The examples on Chart 23 illustrate the point.

If you haven't done very much colour planning before, it is a good idea to study a colour wheel to see how well some colours complement each other, and how others do nothing for one another! Colour wheels are often illustrated in books on learning to paint, so look in the art and craft section of your library. The wheel will show you how the three primary colours – blue, red and yellow – are mixed to produce yet more colours. When black or white is added, further tones and shades are produced. The more planning of colour schemes you do, the more skilled you will become.

CHART 23 PRETTY CIRCLES

CHART 24 MORE FLORAL BORDERS

IDEAS AND ALTERNATIVES

The two pretty borders, above, would look very effective as single motifs, on a greetings card, fridge magnet or a set of glass coasters. You could change the colour schemes again and again, but always copy the design out onto squared paper, similar to that used here, and colour it in so that you can see the effect before you buy your embroidery cottons (floss).

All the designs on Charts 25 and 26 are typical of those found on eighteenth-century samplers. Bands of oak leaves, in particular, were a traditional theme, often accompanied by acorns. Potted plants, stylised and otherwise, were amongst the most popular subjects, whilst roses, carnations and honeysuckle, in many different shapes and forms, were also prolific in samplers of the period. The designs on both of these charts would be ideal if you wanted to make a modern-day sampler in the style of this period.

CHART 25 FLOWERS IN POTS

CHART 26 FLOWERS AND LEAVES

CHART 27 VASE OF FLOWERS

IDEAS AND ALTERNATIVES

The two stylised folk designs on Chart 28 contrast with the lifelike vase of flowers on Chart 27, which has all the glory of an oil painting, and includes some very clever shading on both the vase and the flowers.

The marigolds and chrysanthemums are both sewn in two shades of orange and one of mid olive green, which make a very pleasing colour scheme that is typical of the type of European folk art which is so popular on both sides of the Atlantic.

These designs are just the kind of motif that appears so often on samplers of the eighteenth century, and which would be ideal for a modern-day version. The roses, chrysanthemums and carnations which are consistently repeated in samplers of this period probably owe their popularity to cross stitch, which was the commonest form of embroidery for samplers of this time. Their regular, almost geometric, shapes lend themselves perfectly to interpretation in cross stitch.

If you are just looking for a small subject, either of these designs would make the perfect greetings card. Or better still, make a matching bookmark to accompany your card, using the design twice, the second time reversing it so that the two flowers are base-to-base. You can see examples of two different designs in the photograph of the bookmarks on page 6.

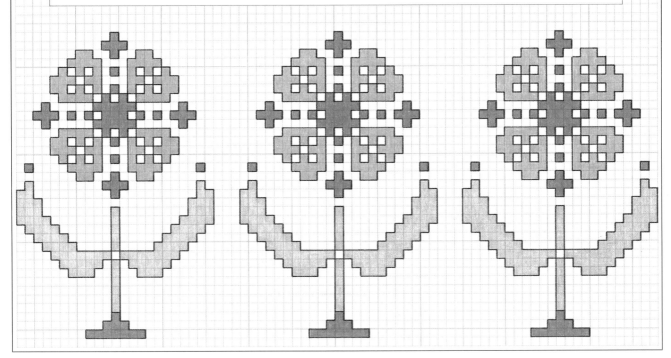

CHART 28 FOLK ART

CHART 29 EYE-CATCHING BORDERS

CHART 30 MORE EYE-CATCHING BORDERS

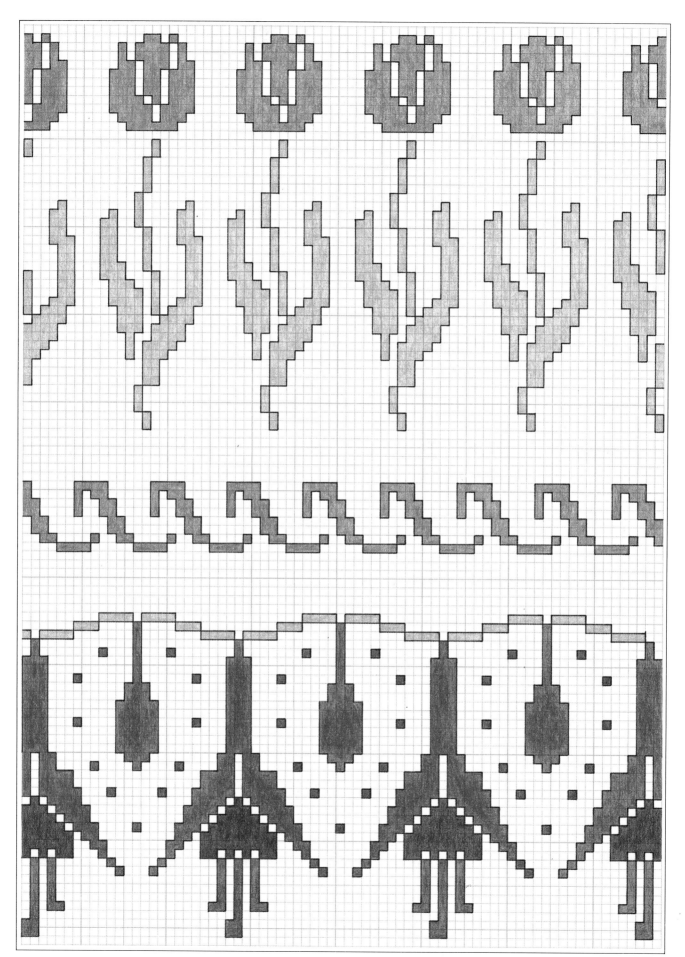

CHART 31 TULIPS AND FUCHSIAS

CHART 32 STILL MORE FLORAL BORDERS

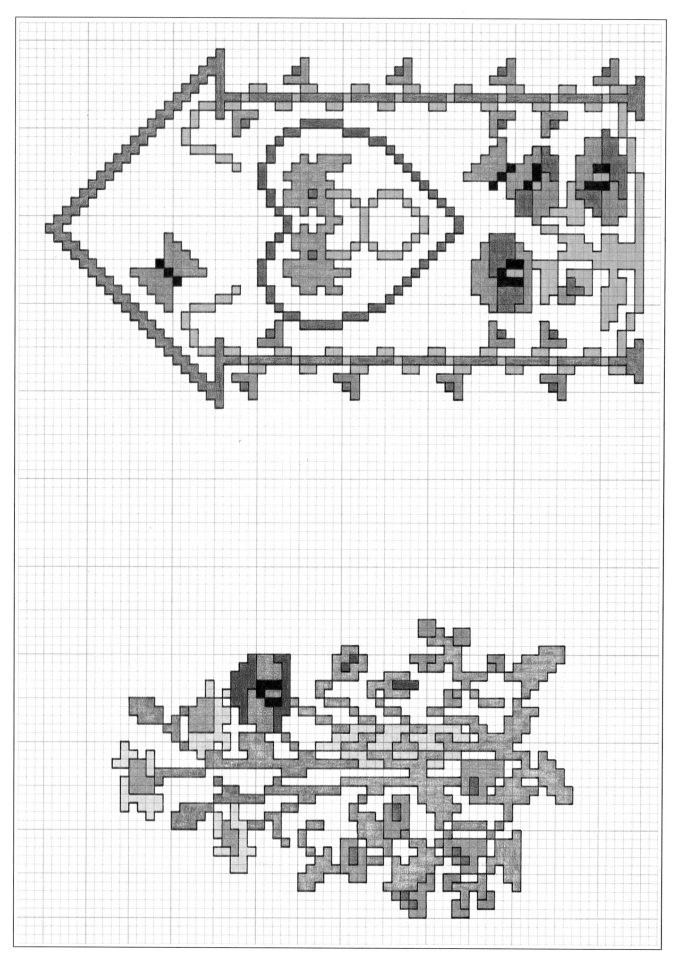

CHART 33 WILD FLOWERS AND A LOVE PAGODA

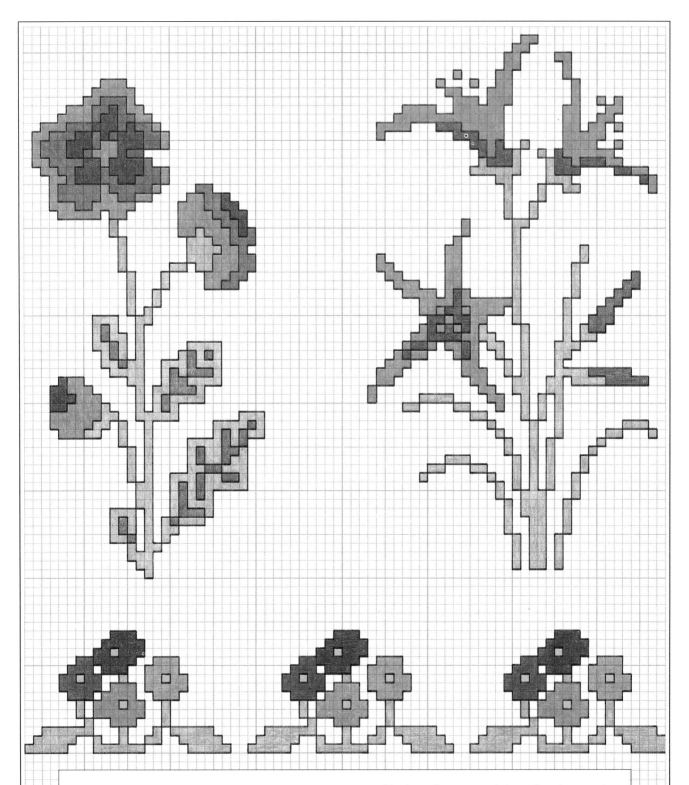

IDEAS AND ALTERNATIVES

The two larger designs on this chart lend themselves to many applications, including a freestyle sampler. But one of the most eye-catching would be a pair of small pictures, set in brass oval, watch-top hanger frames.

These frames are the most superb way to set off your work, and make a really special gift. Once you have pressed your work under a damp cloth and allowed it to dry, the actual framing takes minutes to do. There is a special locking device to seal the embroidery inside, and your work will be completely protected by either clear acetate or flat or convex glass. This covers the stitched piece to protect and enhance the design. The picture frames are finished off with a neat backing on the reverse side.

These gilded metal frames come in various sizes and styles including round and oval ones; a tiny brooch or pendant frame is also available in this range.

CHART 34 FRAMING FLOWERS

IDEAS AND ALTERNATIVES

There is something very intriguing about looking into a window, which is perhaps why this pair of 'window' pictures (Charts 35 and 36) is so fascinating. You can see them embroidered as pictures in the photograph on page 14.

The little flower designs offer plenty of scope to be used individually; greetings cards are an obvious choice. Add a border, similar to the one shown here, to make an attractive frame for each little window pane.

Another attractive idea, this time for the kitchen, is a set of fridge magnets. Either choose different flowers or, just for fun, try embroidering the same flower design but do it in several completely different and contrasting colourways.

Use the border shown here above and below each design, worked all in one colour, to match the kitchen, or pick out one of the predominant colours of the embroidery – perhaps the colour you have already used for each flower pot or vase.   ▷

CHART 35 WINDOW MAGIC

◁ Fridge magnets could not be easier to make up. They are made from clear plastic and all you have to do is press your embroidery, cut it to size, and slide it between the two layers of plastic, where it is instantly gripped. However, to avoid the possibility of the cut edges of the fabric fraying, it is wise to back it with a very thin iron-on Vilene before you cut it to size. This will act as a bonding seal to prevent the threads unravelling.

Tiny gift tags would look lovely with just a single flower – no leaves or pot – set in the centre. Outline the blossom with a single strand of embroidery cotton (floss) in a darker shade than the petals.

Yet another possibility would be a set of glass coasters. Choose from the four designs you like best, and embroider one for each. On the other hand, you could make a set of six square fabric coasters, fringing the edges or turning under a narrow hem. Back them with plain fabric if you want to make them thicker – though the Aida is firm enough not to need backing.

CHART 36 MORE WINDOW MAGIC

CHART 37 FLORAL FOLK DESIGN

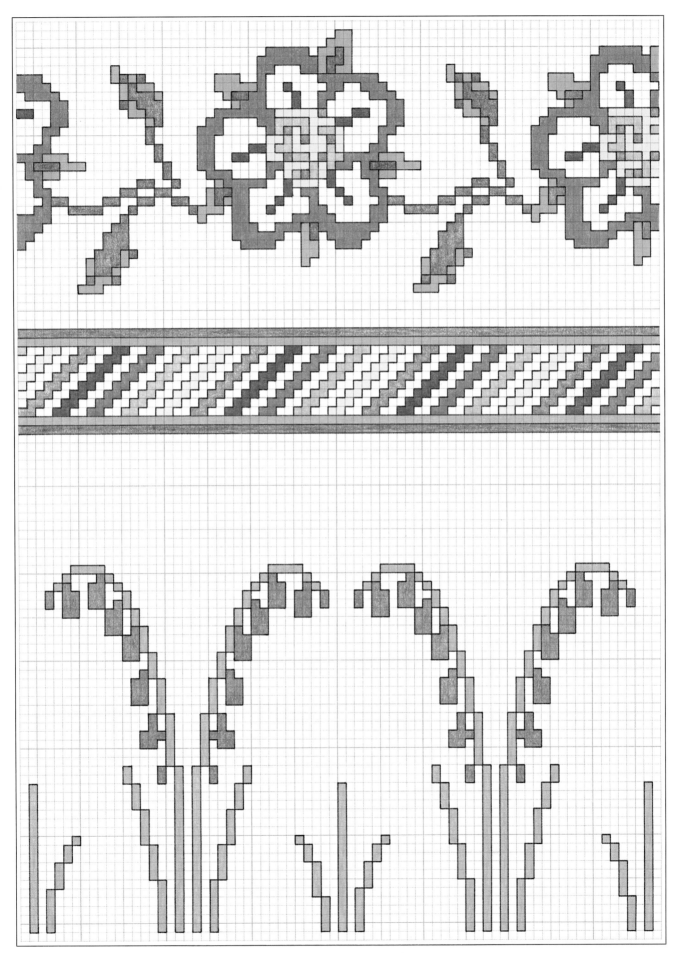

CHART 38 DOG ROSES AND BLUEBELLS

USING THE DESIGN

This unusual study of irises would make a lovely picture, or look stunning if used to cover an address book, telephone index or notebook.

Making a Book Cover

Find a suitable book to cover, then work out how much fabric you will need, taking the fabric round the spine and across the back, allowing about 1in (2.5cm) to overlap round all the edges.

When you have cut the fabric to size, wrap it round the cover to determine the exact area of the front cover – mark the edge with a tacking (basting) thread. Find the centre point and mark it. From this point work out where the design should fall and then begin your embroidery. Worked on 14-count Aida, the design will be just under 4in (10cm) square. When the embroidery is completed, press.

Cover the book carefully, stretching the fabric over the corners by sticking a strip of double-sided tape round the edge, and pressing the fabric onto it. Adjust as necessary, until you get the position right, with the thread of the fabric aligned to the edge of the cover. Turn the surplus round the edges to the inside of the book and trim the fabric to fit. Mitre corners (see Chapter 4) and use a clear adhesive, like UHU, to prevent fraying. Fix the fabric firmly inside the cover with double-sided tape or glue. Mask the cut edges with a piece of paper.

CHART 39 GROWING IRISES

CHART 40 WISE OLD OWL

IDEAS AND ALTERNATIVES

Stylised folk art designs like this one are timeless and provide yet more wonderful material for making samplers – that old-fashioned art which also is as popular today as ever it was. This design can also be seen as a framed picture in the photograph on page 14.

The design could form the large central motif for a traditional eighteenth-century style sampler, with smaller motifs arranged around it. There are plenty of suitable ones on Charts 3, 4, 7, 8, 9, 10, 12, 13, 14, 16, 21, 23, 25, 28, 32, 42, 46 and 47. Although they are mainly floral, do not forget to include animals and birds as well. To complete the work you need a border. There are many lovely designs for a sampler of this type throughout the book, but look particularly at the ones on Charts 2, 5, 6, 42, 48, 49 and 50.

The colour choice for the design is up to you. As the stylised flowers could be any variety of bloom, you are not limited to any particular colour scheme. Just be guided by the suggestions in the examples above, and keep within a definite colour range. For instance, purple and blue, lilac and pink or cream and gold would all work well; the latter suggestion would look stunning on a midnight blue ground, with pale olive leaves and slightly darker stalks.

The ornamental vase is as important as the flowers, so choose a colour for this feature that sets off the floral arrangement. The more colourful the flowers, the more neutral the vase needs to be. Then, if necessary, outline the vase either in a darker shade of the same colour or in black using just one strand of embroidery cotton (floss). You may not need to outline the cut-away sections: this depends on the strength of your vase colour, so be guided by this.

CHART 41 A SAMPLER DESIGN

CHART 42 FLORAL FOLK BORDERS

CHART 43 HEARTS AND FLOWERS

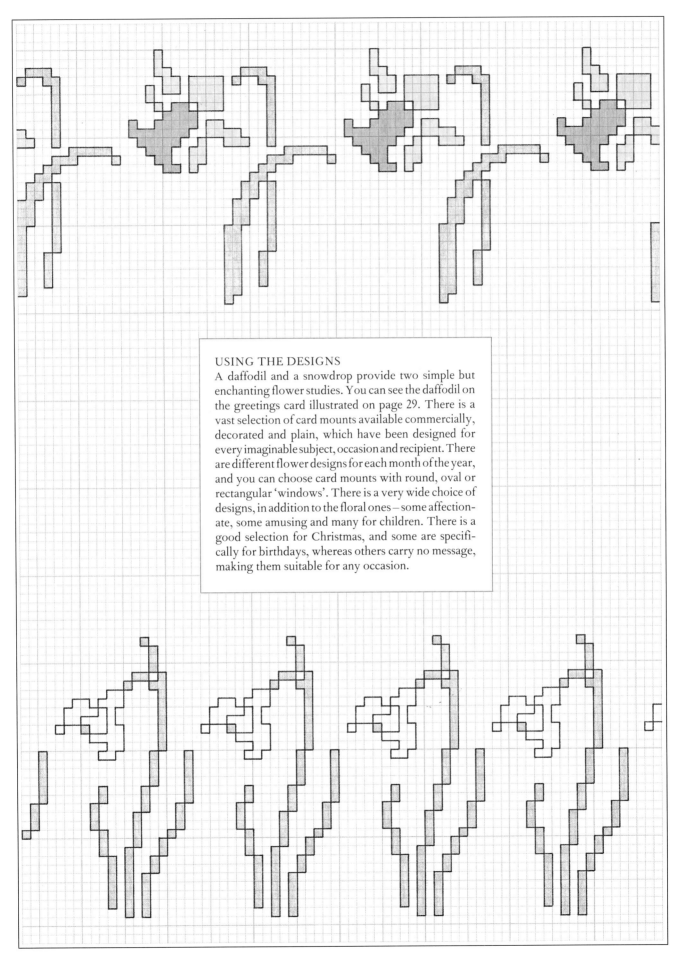

USING THE DESIGNS
A daffodil and a snowdrop provide two simple but enchanting flower studies. You can see the daffodil on the greetings card illustrated on page 29. There is a vast selection of card mounts available commercially, decorated and plain, which have been designed for every imaginable subject, occasion and recipient. There are different flower designs for each month of the year, and you can choose card mounts with round, oval or rectangular 'windows'. There is a very wide choice of designs, in addition to the floral ones – some affectionate, some amusing and many for children. There is a good selection for Christmas, and some are specifically for birthdays, whereas others carry no message, making them suitable for any occasion.

CHART 44 SPRING FLOWERS

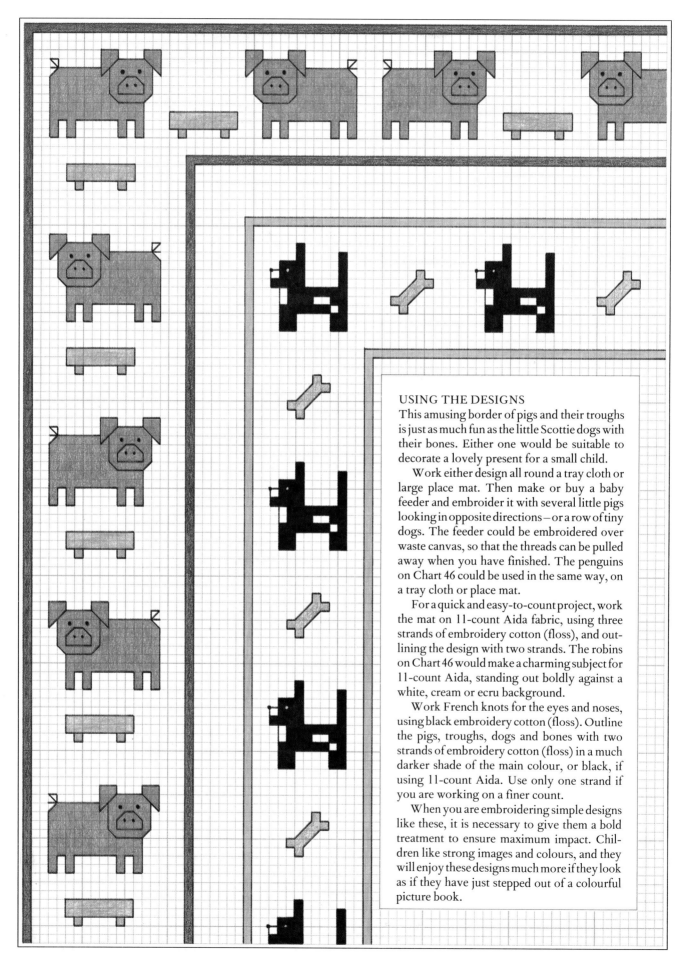

USING THE DESIGNS

This amusing border of pigs and their troughs is just as much fun as the little Scottie dogs with their bones. Either one would be suitable to decorate a lovely present for a small child.

Work either design all round a tray cloth or large place mat. Then make or buy a baby feeder and embroider it with several little pigs looking in opposite directions – or a row of tiny dogs. The feeder could be embroidered over waste canvas, so that the threads can be pulled away when you have finished. The penguins on Chart 46 could be used in the same way, on a tray cloth or place mat.

For a quick and easy-to-count project, work the mat on 11-count Aida fabric, using three strands of embroidery cotton (floss), and outlining the design with two strands. The robins on Chart 46 would make a charming subject for 11-count Aida, standing out boldly against a white, cream or ecru background.

Work French knots for the eyes and noses, using black embroidery cotton (floss). Outline the pigs, troughs, dogs and bones with two strands of embroidery cotton (floss) in a much darker shade of the main colour, or black, if using 11-count Aida. Use only one strand if you are working on a finer count.

When you are embroidering simple designs like these, it is necessary to give them a bold treatment to ensure maximum impact. Children like strong images and colours, and they will enjoy these designs much more if they look as if they have just stepped out of a colourful picture book.

CHART 45 ANIMAL BORDERS

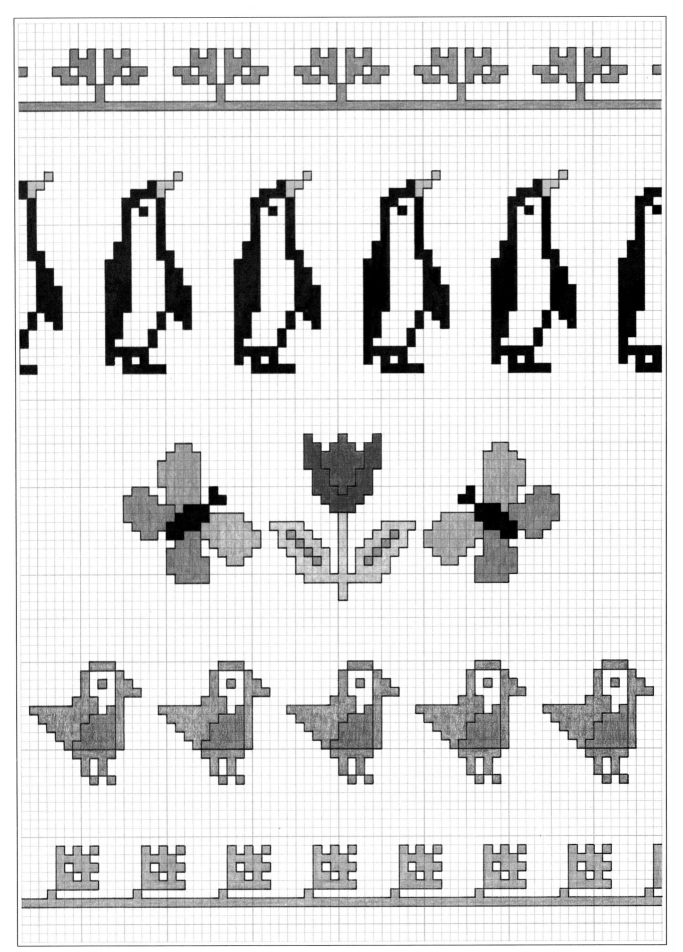

CHART 46 PENGUINS AND ROBINS

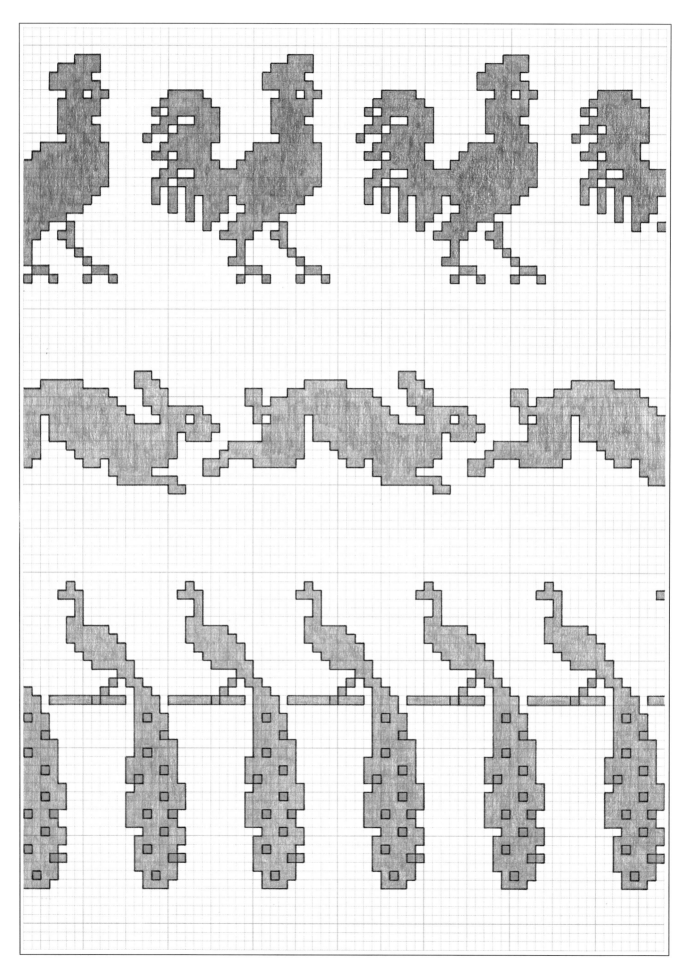

CHART 47 COCKERELS, RABBITS AND PEACOCKS

CHART 48 HEARTS, BUTTERFLIES AND POPPIES

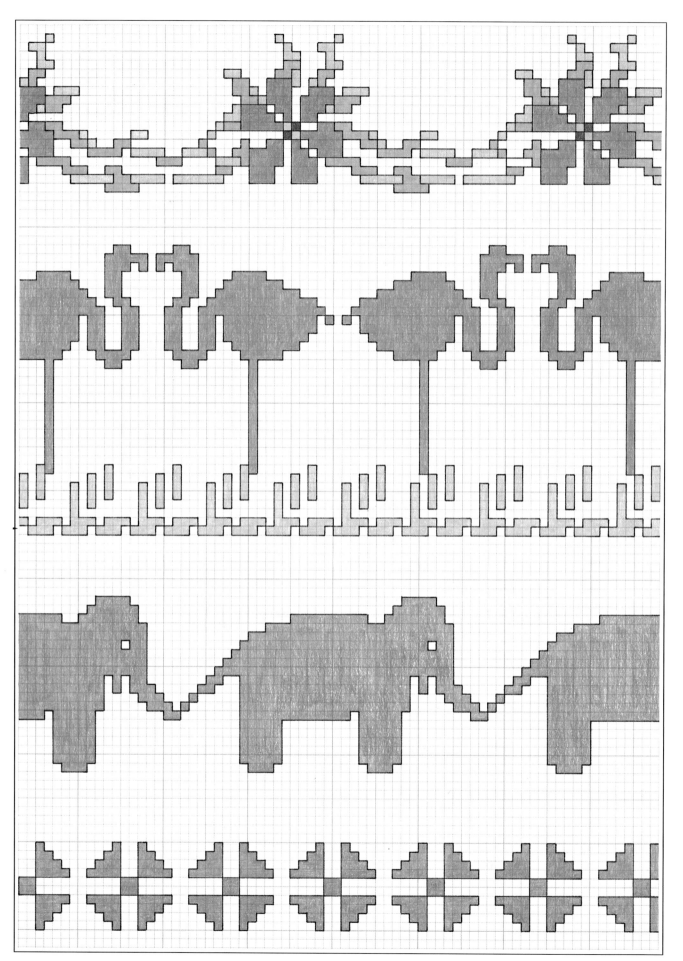

CHART 49 FLOWERS, FLAMINGOES AND ELEPHANTS

CHART 50 PIGS, FISH, BUTTERFLIES AND FLOWERS

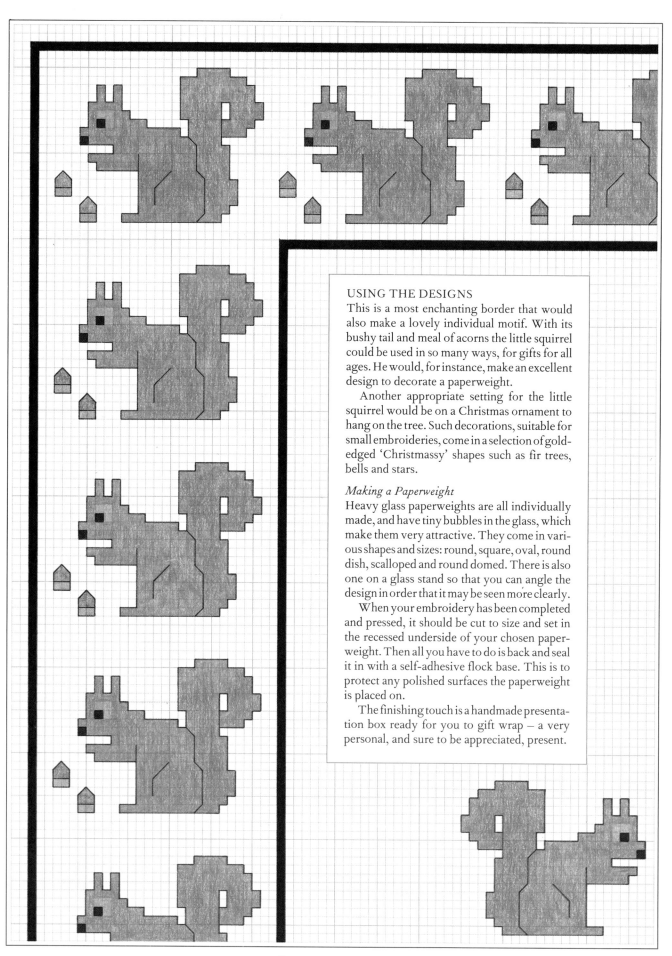

USING THE DESIGNS

This is a most enchanting border that would also make a lovely individual motif. With its bushy tail and meal of acorns the little squirrel could be used in so many ways, for gifts for all ages. He would, for instance, make an excellent design to decorate a paperweight.

Another appropriate setting for the little squirrel would be on a Christmas ornament to hang on the tree. Such decorations, suitable for small embroideries, come in a selection of gold-edged 'Christmassy' shapes such as fir trees, bells and stars.

Making a Paperweight

Heavy glass paperweights are all individually made, and have tiny bubbles in the glass, which make them very attractive. They come in various shapes and sizes: round, square, oval, round dish, scalloped and round domed. There is also one on a glass stand so that you can angle the design in order that it may be seen more clearly.

When your embroidery has been completed and pressed, it should be cut to size and set in the recessed underside of your chosen paperweight. Then all you have to do is back and seal it in with a self-adhesive flock base. This is to protect any polished surfaces the paperweight is placed on.

The finishing touch is a handmade presentation box ready for you to gift wrap – a very personal, and sure to be appreciated, present.

CHART 51 SQUIRRELS AND ACORNS

CHART 52 BUSH BABIES, TURTLES, RABBITS AND FISH

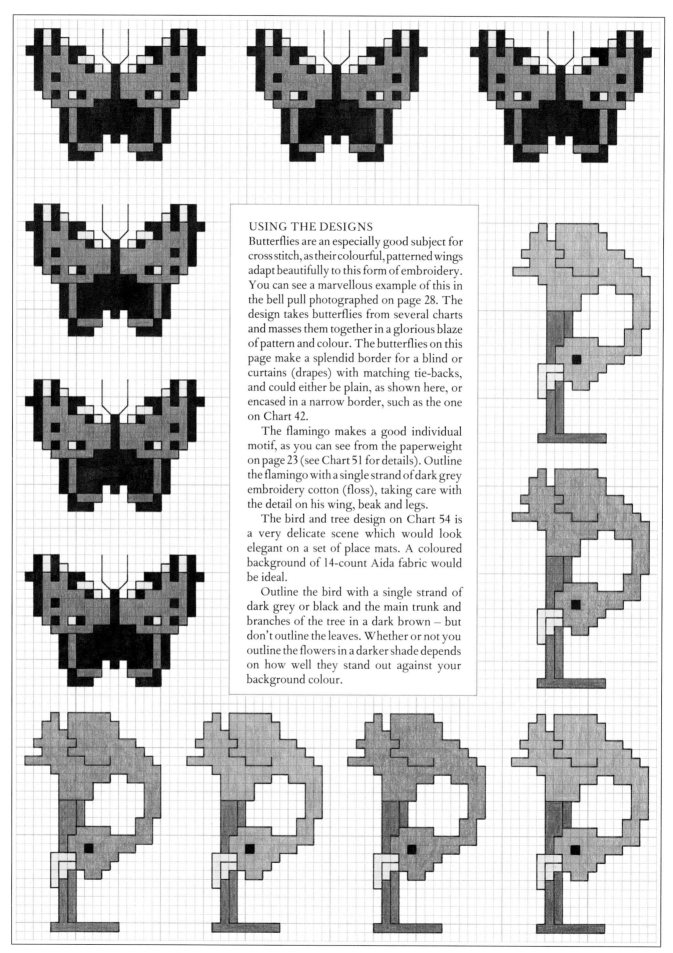

USING THE DESIGNS

Butterflies are an especially good subject for cross stitch, as their colourful, patterned wings adapt beautifully to this form of embroidery. You can see a marvellous example of this in the bell pull photographed on page 28. The design takes butterflies from several charts and masses them together in a glorious blaze of pattern and colour. The butterflies on this page make a splendid border for a blind or curtains (drapes) with matching tie-backs, and could either be plain, as shown here, or encased in a narrow border, such as the one on Chart 42.

The flamingo makes a good individual motif, as you can see from the paperweight on page 23 (see Chart 51 for details). Outline the flamingo with a single strand of dark grey embroidery cotton (floss), taking care with the detail on his wing, beak and legs.

The bird and tree design on Chart 54 is a very delicate scene which would look elegant on a set of place mats. A coloured background of 14-count Aida fabric would be ideal.

Outline the bird with a single strand of dark grey or black and the main trunk and branches of the tree in a dark brown – but don't outline the leaves. Whether or not you outline the flowers in a darker shade depends on how well they stand out against your background colour.

CHART 53 BUTTERFLIES AND BIRDS

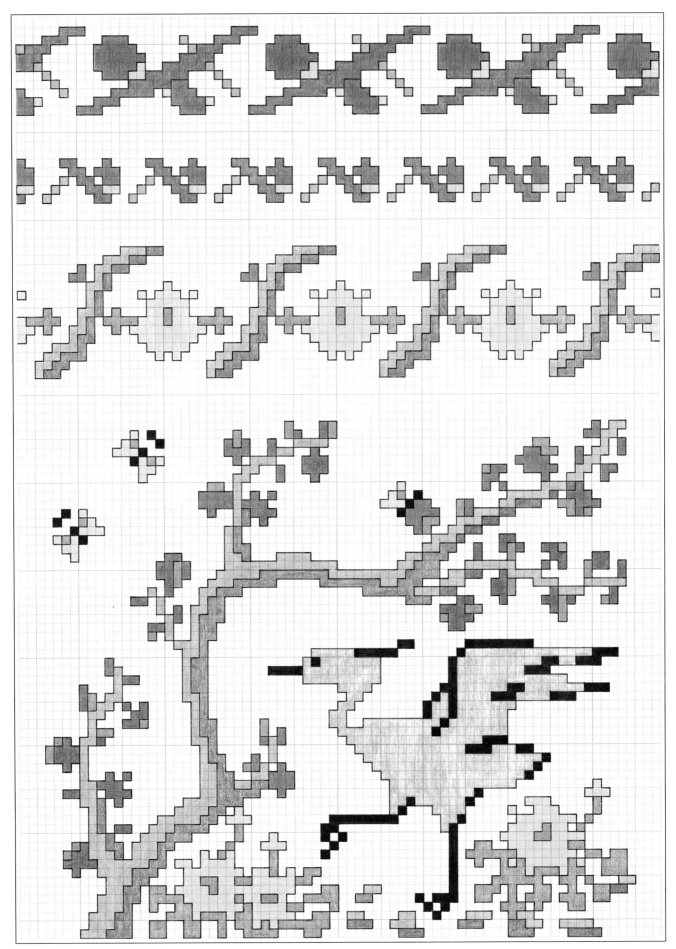

CHART 54 CHINESE BORDERS AND BIRD

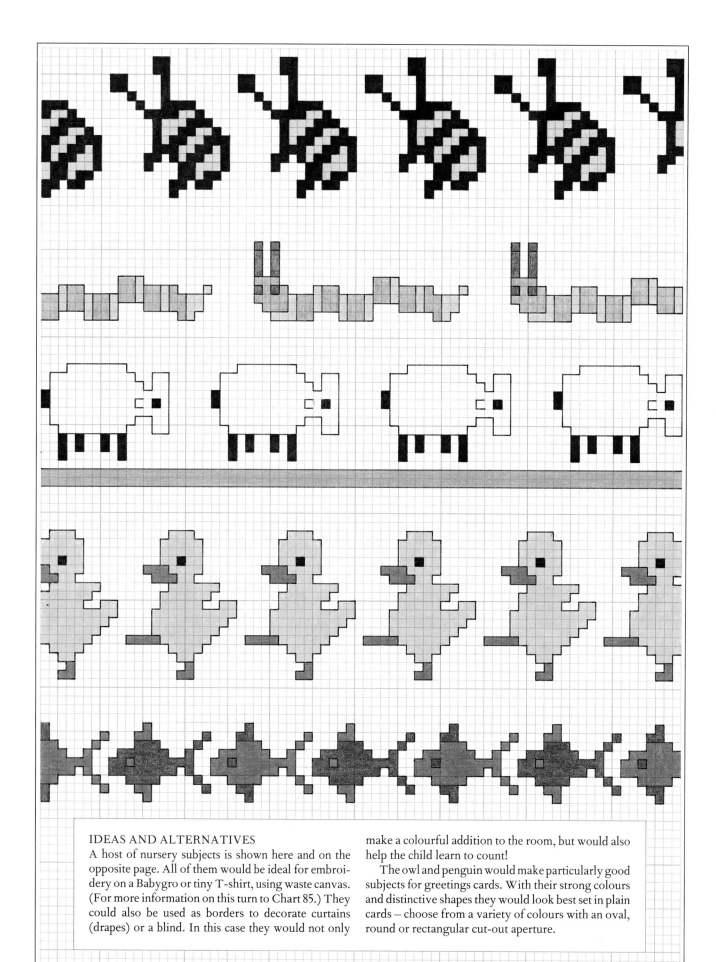

IDEAS AND ALTERNATIVES

A host of nursery subjects is shown here and on the opposite page. All of them would be ideal for embroidery on a Babygro or tiny T-shirt, using waste canvas. (For more information on this turn to Chart 85.) They could also be used as borders to decorate curtains (drapes) or a blind. In this case they would not only make a colourful addition to the room, but would also help the child learn to count!

The owl and penguin would make particularly good subjects for greetings cards. With their strong colours and distinctive shapes they would look best set in plain cards – choose from a variety of colours with an oval, round or rectangular cut-out aperture.

CHART 55 CHILDREN IN MIND

CHART 56 FROM PUPPIES TO PENGUINS

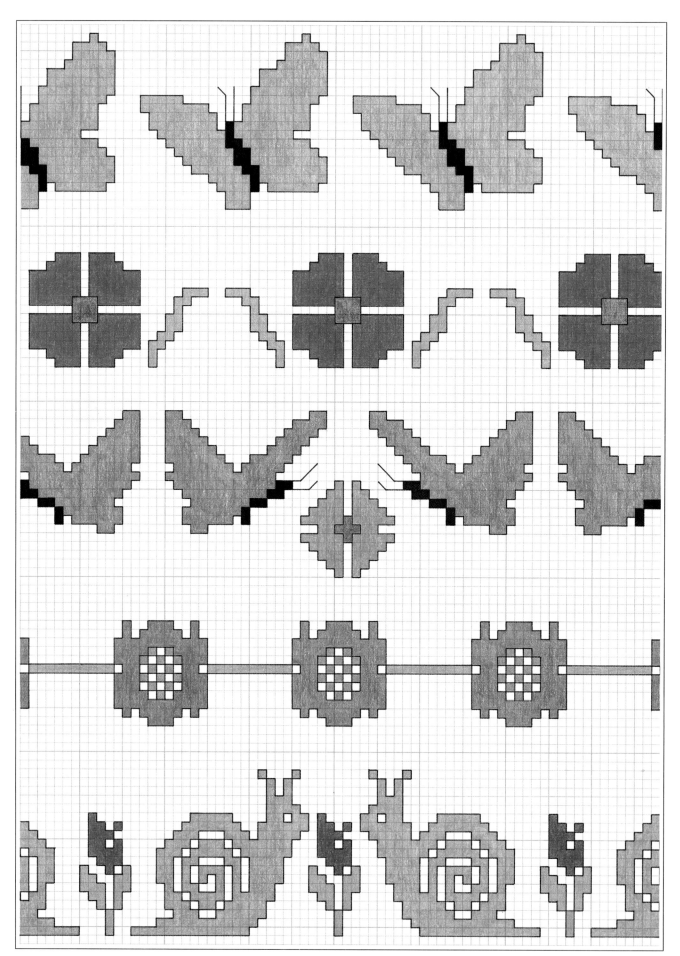

CHART 57 BUTTERFLIES, FLOWERS AND SNAILS

USING THE DESIGN

Framing a Photograph

First decide on a measurement for the inner and outer edges of the frame. The inner measurement must be a little smaller than your mirror or photograph, so that the frame overlaps. The width of the frame should suit the size of the mirror or photograph. Use a piece of paper to visualise the finished effect. Work out the design carefully on graph paper before you start. With 14-count Aida, you will need fourteen squares of graph paper in each direction for every square inch. When you have marked the area of the frame on the paper, fill in the design, adjusting to fit.

Cut your fabric at least 1¼in (3cm) larger all round than the finished frame, and mark the position of the inner and outer edges with a tacking (basting) thread. Embroider the design. When it is finished, make up like the mount for a framed picture (follow the guidelines on Charts 109 and 110). Finish with a strut at the back so that it will stand, or a fine cord for hanging.

CHART 58 BORDERS FOR FRAMES

IDEAS AND ALTERNATIVES

Starfish are an obvious choice for the bathroom, embroidered on Aida bands with a blue edge.

Work the snails on 14-count Aida for a delicate effect, or 11-count for a bolder one. Outline in a darker shade of the main colour. Back with fabric to make a simple coverlet – or lightweight wadding (batting) for a cosy quilt.

The little lion would make a charming birthday card – outline the body with the mane colour and the mane with dark brown – and the bunnies (Chart 60) would be delightful in pale grey on a pair of curtains.

CHART 59 MORE BORDERS

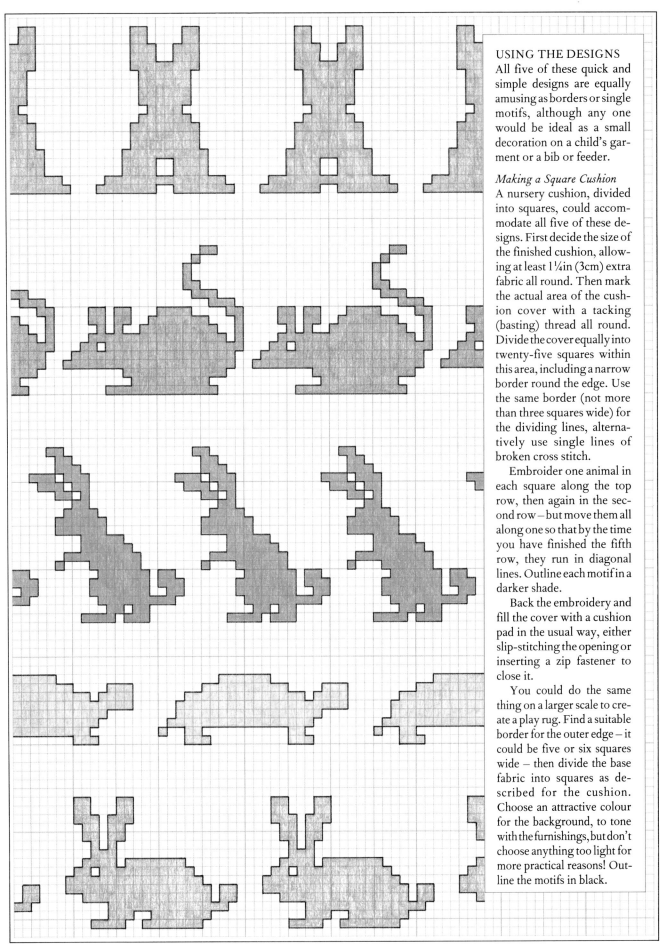

USING THE DESIGNS

All five of these quick and simple designs are equally amusing as borders or single motifs, although any one would be ideal as a small decoration on a child's garment or a bib or feeder.

Making a Square Cushion
A nursery cushion, divided into squares, could accommodate all five of these designs. First decide the size of the finished cushion, allowing at least 1¼in (3cm) extra fabric all round. Then mark the actual area of the cushion cover with a tacking (basting) thread all round. Divide the cover equally into twenty-five squares within this area, including a narrow border round the edge. Use the same border (not more than three squares wide) for the dividing lines, alternatively use single lines of broken cross stitch.

Embroider one animal in each square along the top row, then again in the second row – but move them all along one so that by the time you have finished the fifth row, they run in diagonal lines. Outline each motif in a darker shade.

Back the embroidery and fill the cover with a cushion pad in the usual way, either slip-stitching the opening or inserting a zip fastener to close it.

You could do the same thing on a larger scale to create a play rug. Find a suitable border for the outer edge – it could be five or six squares wide – then divide the base fabric into squares as described for the cushion. Choose an attractive colour for the background, to tone with the furnishings, but don't choose anything too light for more practical reasons! Outline the motifs in black.

CHART 60 ANIMALS TO COUNT ON

CHART 61 SCOTTIES, MICE, FRUIT AND BUTTERFLIES

CHART 62 ROBINS, SNAILS AND PLAYFUL PUPS

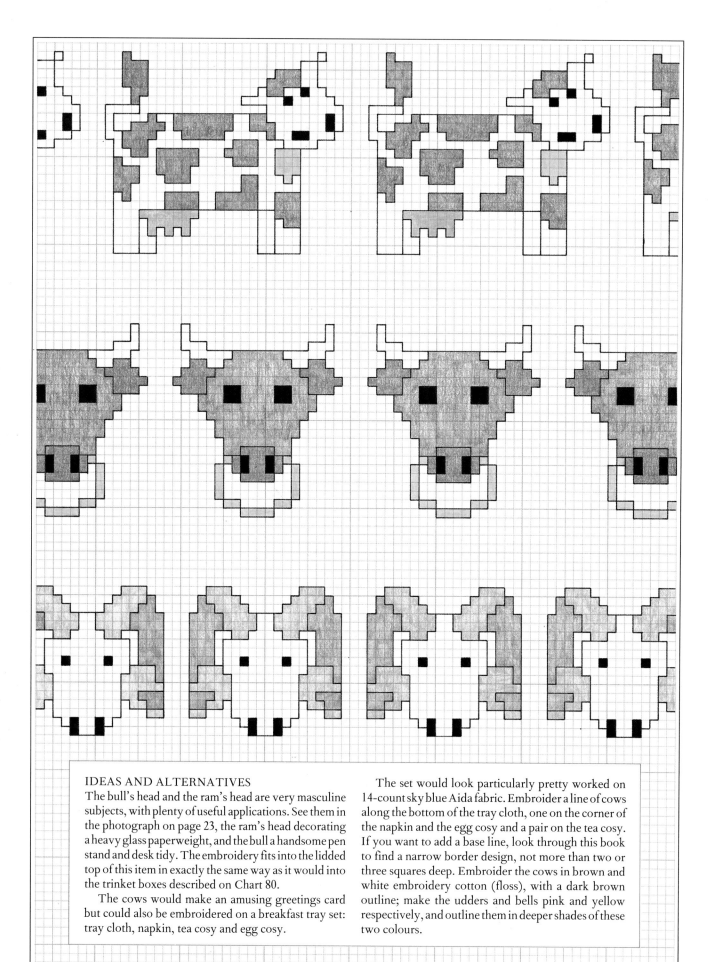

IDEAS AND ALTERNATIVES

The bull's head and the ram's head are very masculine subjects, with plenty of useful applications. See them in the photograph on page 23, the ram's head decorating a heavy glass paperweight, and the bull a handsome pen stand and desk tidy. The embroidery fits into the lidded top of this item in exactly the same way as it would into the trinket boxes described on Chart 80.

The cows would make an amusing greetings card but could also be embroidered on a breakfast tray set: tray cloth, napkin, tea cosy and egg cosy.

The set would look particularly pretty worked on 14-count sky blue Aida fabric. Embroider a line of cows along the bottom of the tray cloth, one on the corner of the napkin and the egg cosy and a pair on the tea cosy. If you want to add a base line, look through this book to find a narrow border design, not more than two or three squares deep. Embroider the cows in brown and white embroidery cotton (floss), with a dark brown outline; make the udders and bells pink and yellow respectively, and outline them in deeper shades of these two colours.

CHART 63 WITH MEN IN MIND

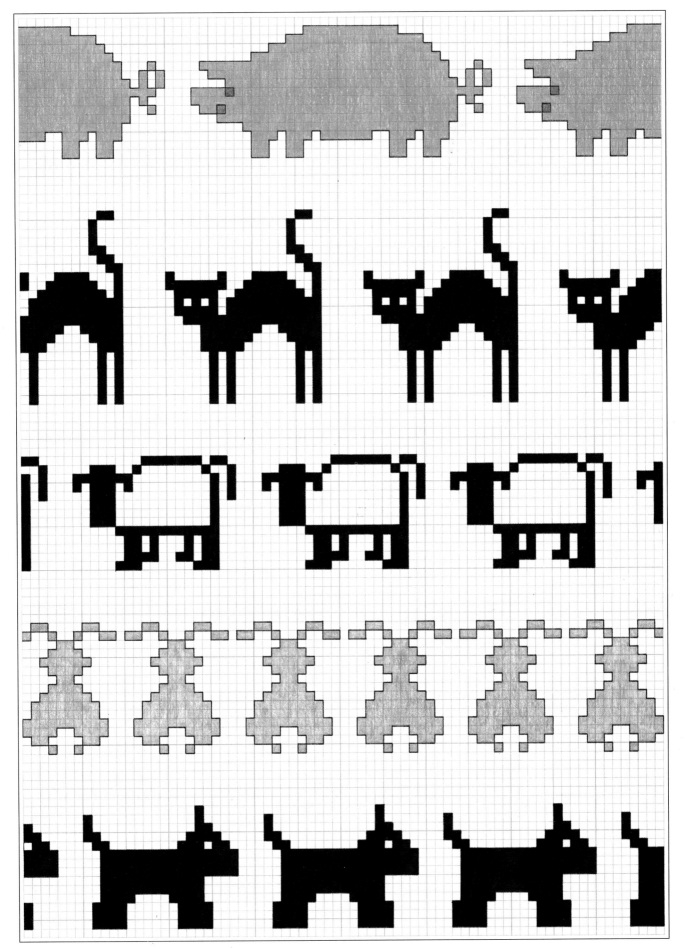

CHART 64 FIVE FRIENDLY ANIMALS

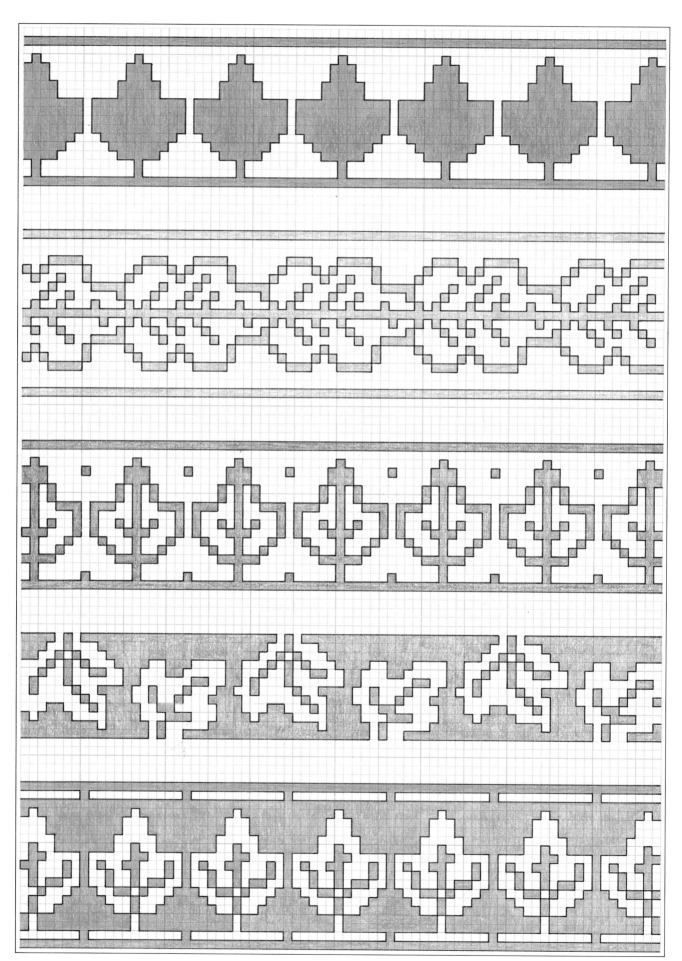

CHART 65 LEAF BORDERS

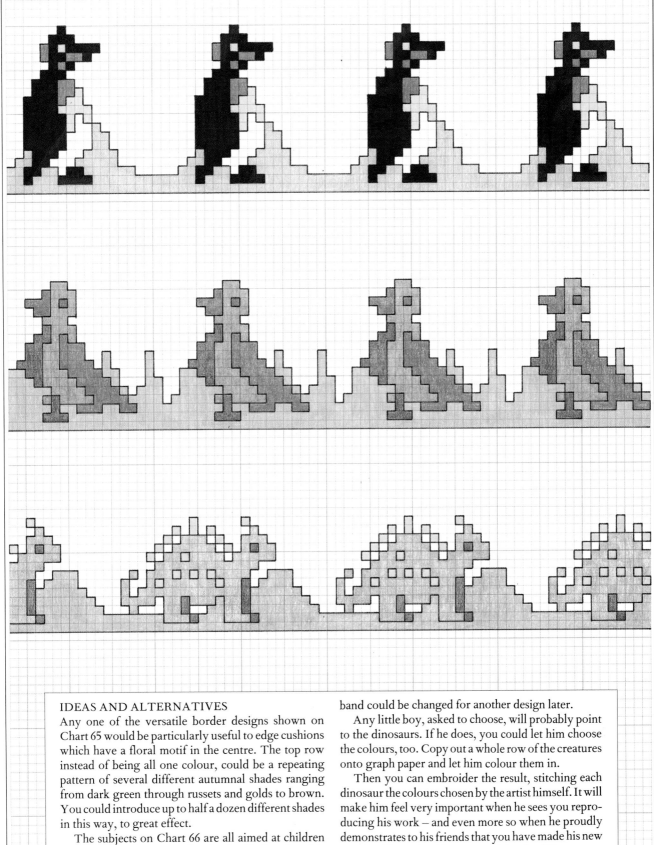

Any one of the versatile border designs shown on Chart 65 would be particularly useful to edge cushions which have a floral motif in the centre. The top row instead of being all one colour, could be a repeating pattern of several different autumnal shades ranging from dark green through russets and golds to brown. You could introduce up to half a dozen different shades in this way, to great effect.

The subjects on Chart 66 are all aimed at children and are ideal for use with edged Aida bands. This would be a quick and easy way to decorate plain curtains (drapes) for a child's room, especially as the band could be changed for another design later.

Any little boy, asked to choose, will probably point to the dinosaurs. If he does, you could let him choose the colours, too. Copy out a whole row of the creatures onto graph paper and let him colour them in.

Then you can embroider the result, stitching each dinosaur the colours chosen by the artist himself. It will make him feel very important when he sees you reproducing his work – and even more so when he proudly demonstrates to his friends that you have made his new curtains (drapes) to his own special orders! For greater emphasis, outline each dinosaur with a single strand of black but do not outline the rocky background.

CHART 66 CHILDREN'S BORDERS

IDEAS AND ALTERNATIVES

If your pet has a habit of walking all over everything and leaving his or her paw prints behind, you will appreciate the design above! Embroider a cushion for your pet's basket, using small pieces of waste canvas to make a track across, or all round it.

Make the cushion itself from something practical and easy to wash, like a heavy cotton poplin. Decide the position of the paw prints, marking each with a pin.

Now tack (baste) on a small piece of waste canvas, at least 14 × 14 squares of mesh in area, over each marked point. Use three strands of cotton (floss) for the embroidery. When the stitching is completed, dampen and remove the threads of canvas in the usual way.

All the motifs on Chart 68 are ideal for a small greetings card. If you want to add a little colour, look through the book for a suitable narrow border, or use just the outer three squares of the border on Chart 71.

CHART 67 EVEN MORE BORDERS

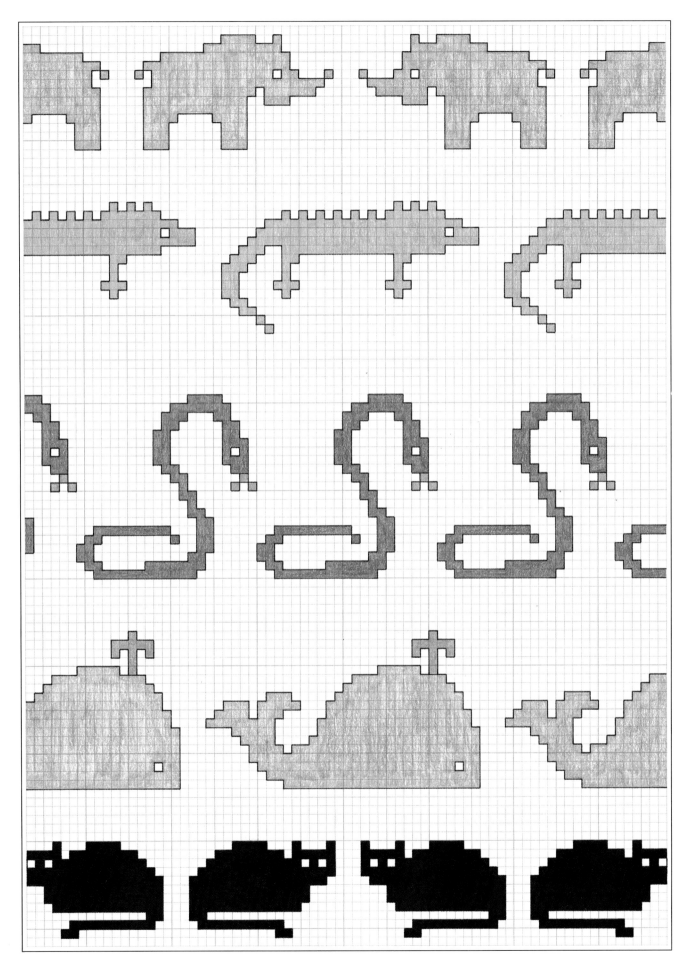

CHART 68 ANIMAL BORDERS

IDEAS AND ALTERNATIVES

Cross stitch is a form of embroidery that children can learn to do quickly and easily. There is so little to learn, and the results are so immediate, that they don't have time to get bored or disillusioned.

All through this book there are designs that are ideal for getting children started: the little birds and hedgehogs shown here are a good example as they are easy to stitch and to follow from the chart. It is a good idea to copy the design out onto larger squares, such as arithmetic book paper for example. This will make it easier for the child to see, and he or she will not be confused by the other designs on this page.

When these two designs have been satisfactorily accomplished, try the upper border of two-tone butterflies, followed by the lower butterflies, which would provide an exercise in backstitch and outlining.

Start children off with a low-count fabric: 8-count or 11-count Aida would be best, giving eight and eleven stitches to the inch respectively. They will need to use three strands of embroidery cotton (floss) on either of these fabrics. Very small children could start on 6-count Binca, which gives only six crosses to the inch: on this they could use a big needle and all six strands of cotton (floss). Or, instead of stranded cottons (floss), use soft embroidery cotton (floss), which comes in 10⅞yd (10 metre) skeins in a wide variety of colours.

CHART 69 STARTING YOUNG

CHART 70 SCARABS, DUCKS, BEES AND SPIDERS

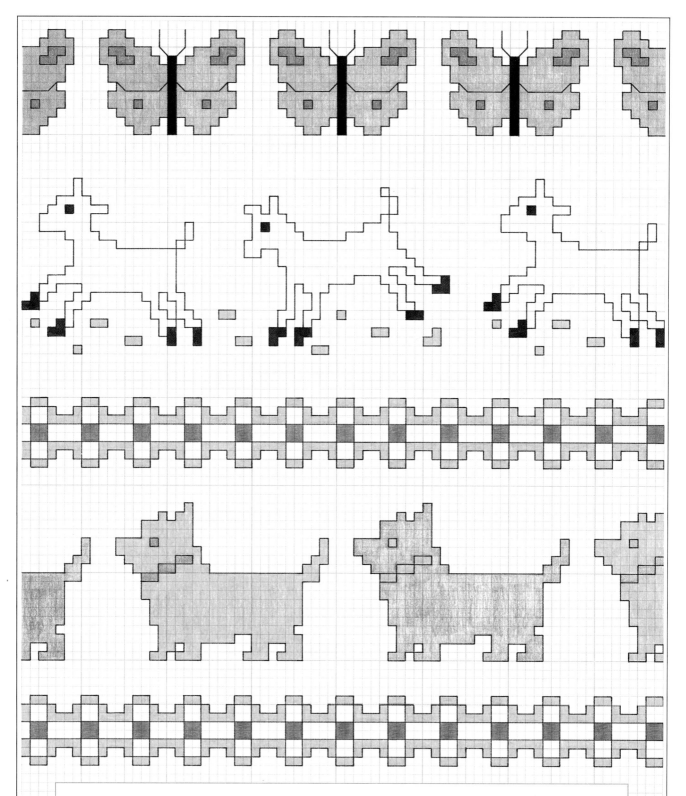

USING THE DESIGNS

Use the subjects on Charts 70, 71 and 72 individually on small greetings cards or gift tags.

Press your embroidery under a damp cloth and allow it to dry thoroughly. Then very carefully measure the position you want it to occupy in the frame of the card mount. When you have decided this, cut the embroidery to size. It should be smaller than the card but a little larger than the cut-out window.

Fix the embroidery behind the aperture with adhesive tape or clear adhesive. If you prefer you can fix your work to the flap behind the aperture, but this tends to create a shadow round the edge.

Finally, close the inner flap back over the fabric so that your work is completely enclosed and the back hidden.

CHART 71 HEARTFELT GREETINGS

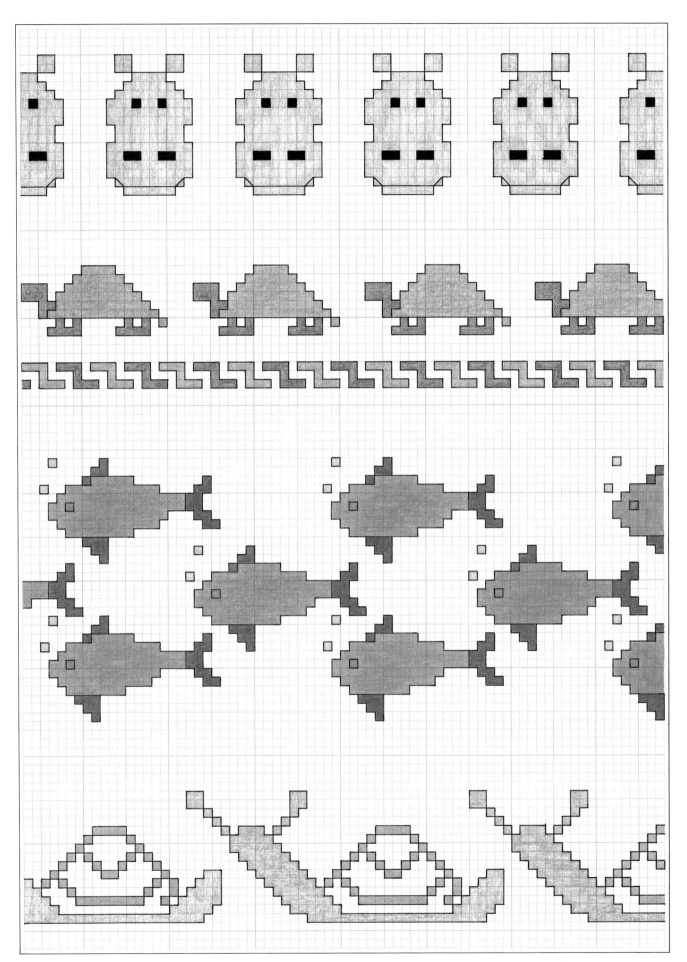

CHART 72 HIPPOS, TORTOISES, FISH AND SNAILS

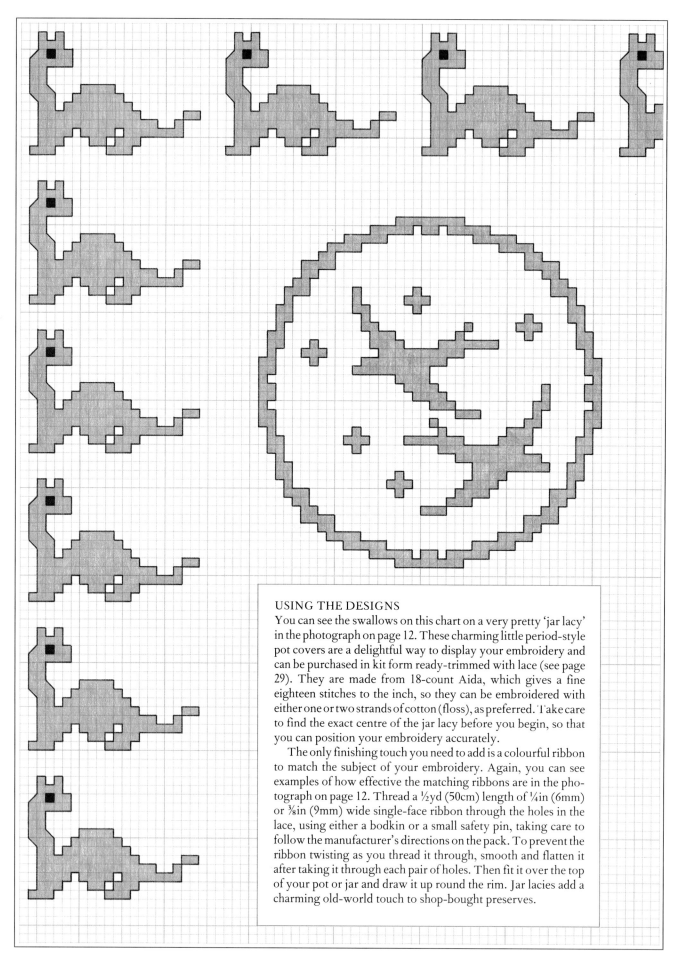

USING THE DESIGNS

You can see the swallows on this chart on a very pretty 'jar lacy' in the photograph on page 12. These charming little period-style pot covers are a delightful way to display your embroidery and can be purchased in kit form ready-trimmed with lace (see page 29). They are made from 18-count Aida, which gives a fine eighteen stitches to the inch, so they can be embroidered with either one or two strands of cotton (floss), as preferred. Take care to find the exact centre of the jar lacy before you begin, so that you can position your embroidery accurately.

The only finishing touch you need to add is a colourful ribbon to match the subject of your embroidery. Again, you can see examples of how effective the matching ribbons are in the photograph on page 12. Thread a ½yd (50cm) length of ¼in (6mm) or ⅜in (9mm) wide single-face ribbon through the holes in the lace, using either a bodkin or a small safety pin, taking care to follow the manufacturer's directions on the pack. To prevent the ribbon twisting as you thread it through, smooth and flatten it after taking it through each pair of holes. Then fit it over the top of your pot or jar and draw it up round the rim. Jar lacies add a charming old-world touch to shop-bought preserves.

CHART 73 SWALLOWS AND DINOSAURS

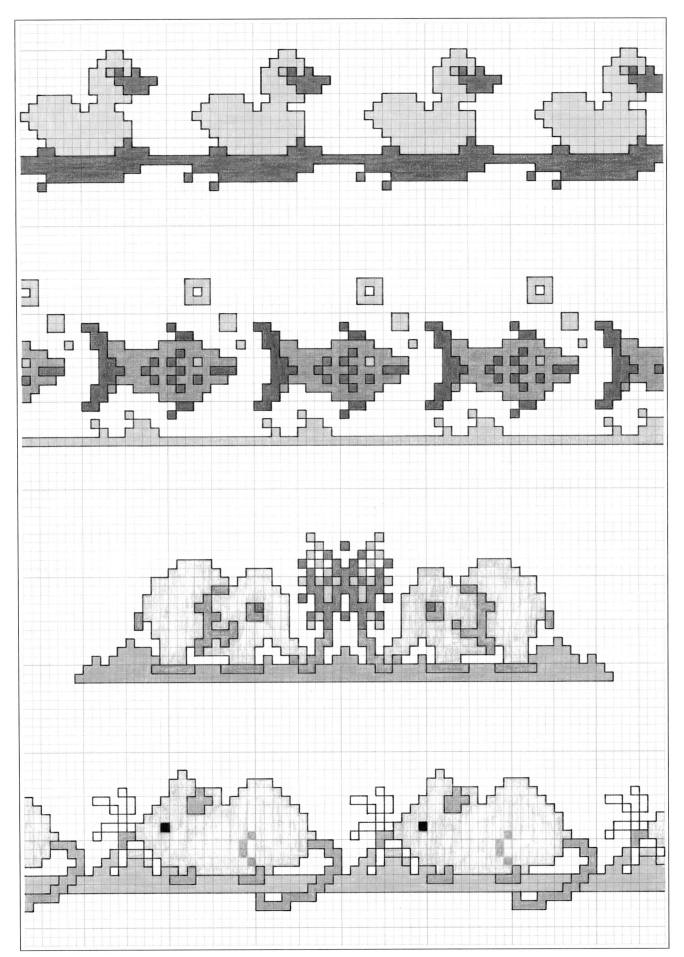

CHART 74 DUCKS, FISH, ELEPHANTS AND MICE

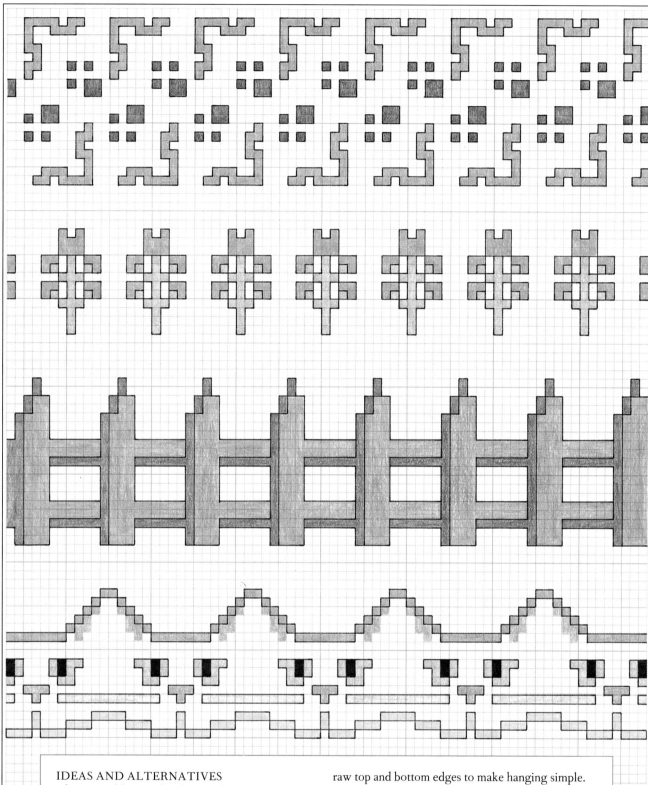

IDEAS AND ALTERNATIVES

The top and bottom borders on this chart are for cat lovers everywhere! Either one would be perfect embroidered on an Aida band and applied to curtains (drapes), towels, shelves, etc. The bands would even look good on a hat!

Apart from all their other uses, the widest bands are ideal for wall hangings and bell pulls, avoiding the need to hem the side edges. All you have to do is turn over the raw top and bottom edges to make hanging simple.

The hedgehog family and the badger on Chart 76 are particularly charming, and could have a lot of applications. As well as the borders shown here, they would make ideal subjects for samplers, which often feature animals and birds as well as flowers.

This type of sampler reached the peak of its popularity in the eighteenth century, and there are examples still in existence today.

CHART 75 PURRS AND PAWS

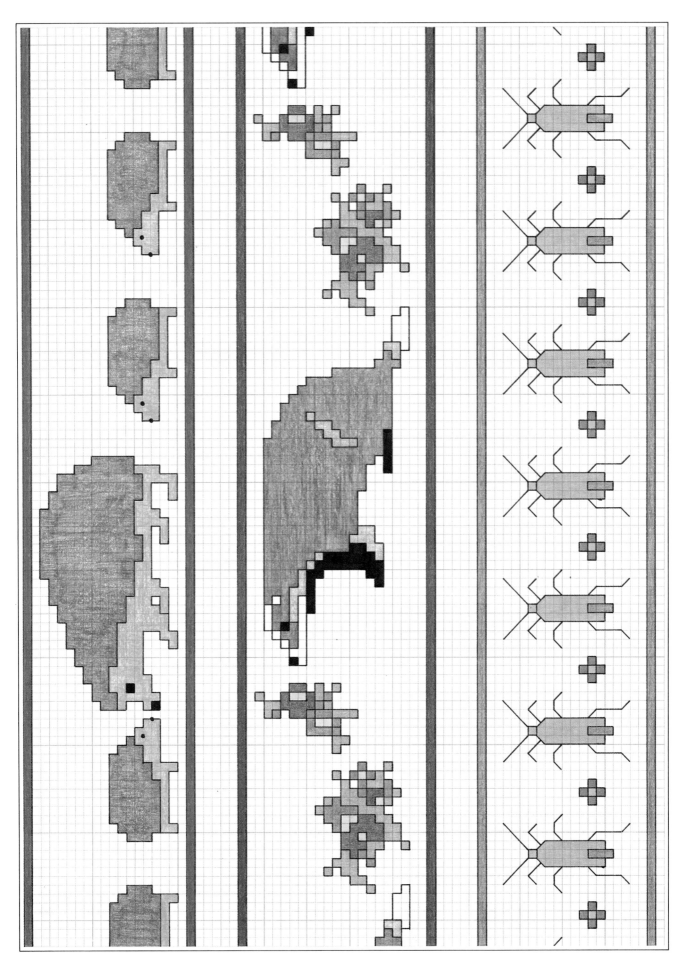

CHART 76 HEDGEHOGS, BADGERS AND BUGS

CHART 77 DOGS AND FOXES

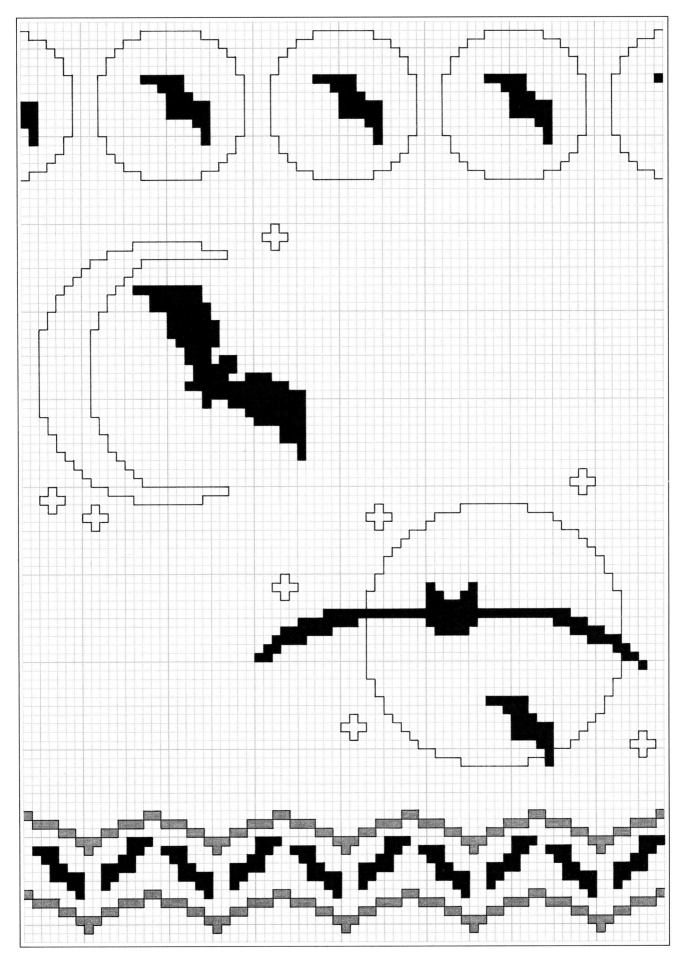

CHART 78 FLYING BATS

CHART 79 ART NOUVEAU BORDERS

Exotic butterflies make a colourful choice for a greetings card, and are charming as a miniature picture.

But they do look wonderful set into the lid of a porcelain trinket box, as you can see in the photograph on page 25. The boxes come in an excellent range of sizes in three different shapes: round, oval and heart-shaped, and in a variety of colours such as ivory, pink, blue, dark green and black.

These boxes can be used anywhere from the bedroom to the living room. On a dressing table they can protect anything from jewellery to face powder. On a desk they keep pins, paper clips, and stamps tidy, whilst on a coffee table they will hold sugared almonds or mints. The needlewoman will find one invaluable for small items, from machine accessories to her tape measure. And for a man, they are ideal for anything from cuff links to loose change.

For something even more special, there are similar bowls in hand-cut lead crystal, and shallow, round boxes plated with silver or gilded.

CHART 80 BUTTERFLIES AND BOXES

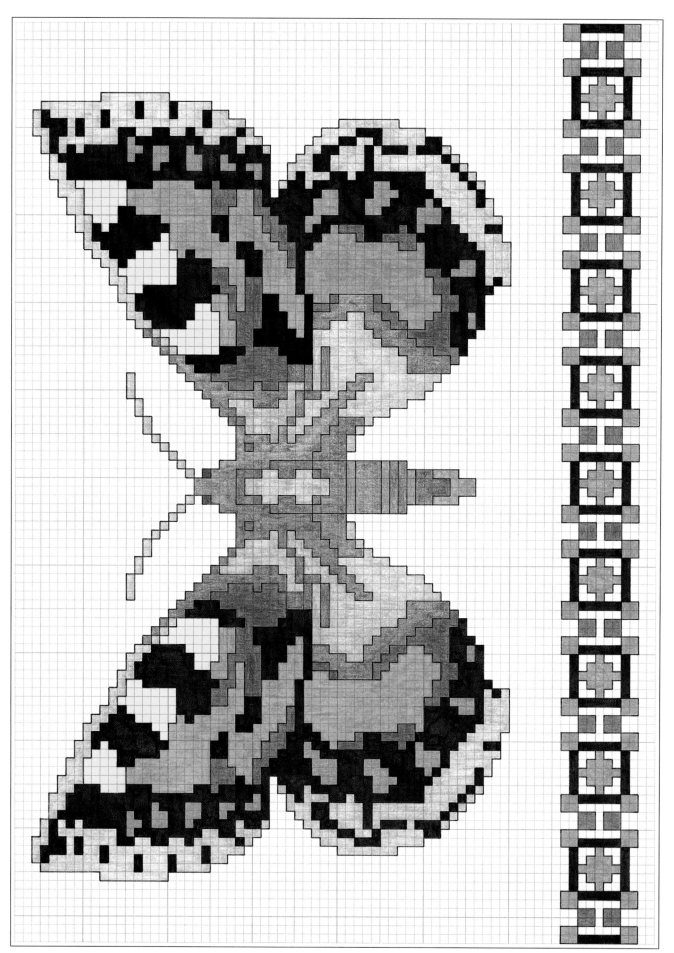

CHART 81 BUTTERFLY AND BORDERS

CHART 82 MORE BUTTERFLIES

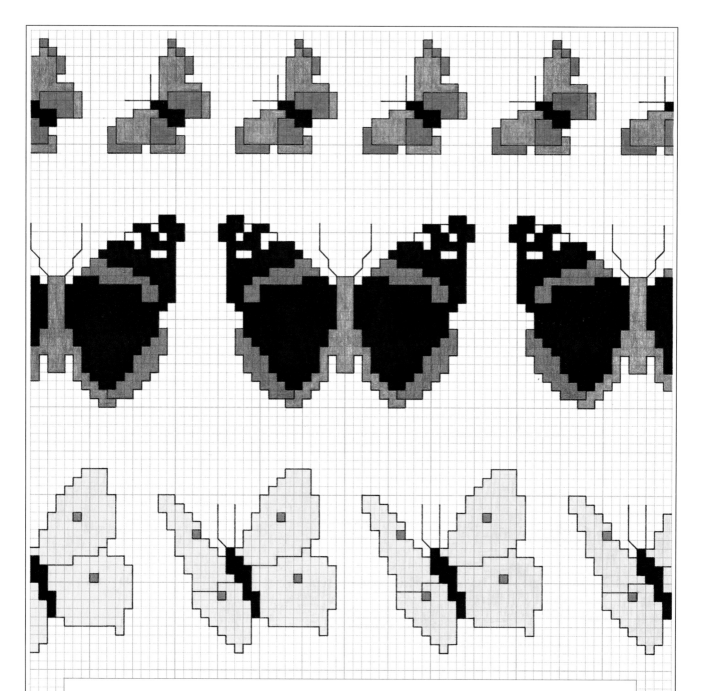

IDEAS AND ALTERNATIVES

Butterflies are a popular theme and any of those on Charts 83 and 84 – particularly the large ones – would make an elegant set of glass coasters. These coasters come in a box of four, and are very easy to make up. Just press the embroidery, cut it to size, insert it in the recessed underside of the coaster and seal it in with the special self-adhesive thick flock base that is designed to protect polished surfaces.

These butterflies would also look most impressive set in the base of heavy glass paperweights, which come in a variety of different shapes, such as round, square and dish, and sizes which range from just over 2in (5cm) to 3in (7.5cm) in diameter. Both the coasters and paperweights are assembled in the same way and have their own handmade presentation boxes.

The polar bear on the chart opposite could hardly be more different! Work him as a small picture, embroidering both the bear and the icebergs in pure white on a coloured ground. Your chosen fabric could be a subtle shade or a strong contrast, for example, sky blue or navy.

Whatever colour scheme you choose, outline the bear and icebergs with a single strand of black (if you are working on 14-count Aida) – and don't forget that single pink stitch for his inner ear. Outline this with a deeper shade of pink. It would also be a good idea to outline the eye and nose in black, to give them greater emphasis. This picture would look particularly attractive framed with a coloured mount.

CHART 83 EVEN MORE BUTTERFLIES

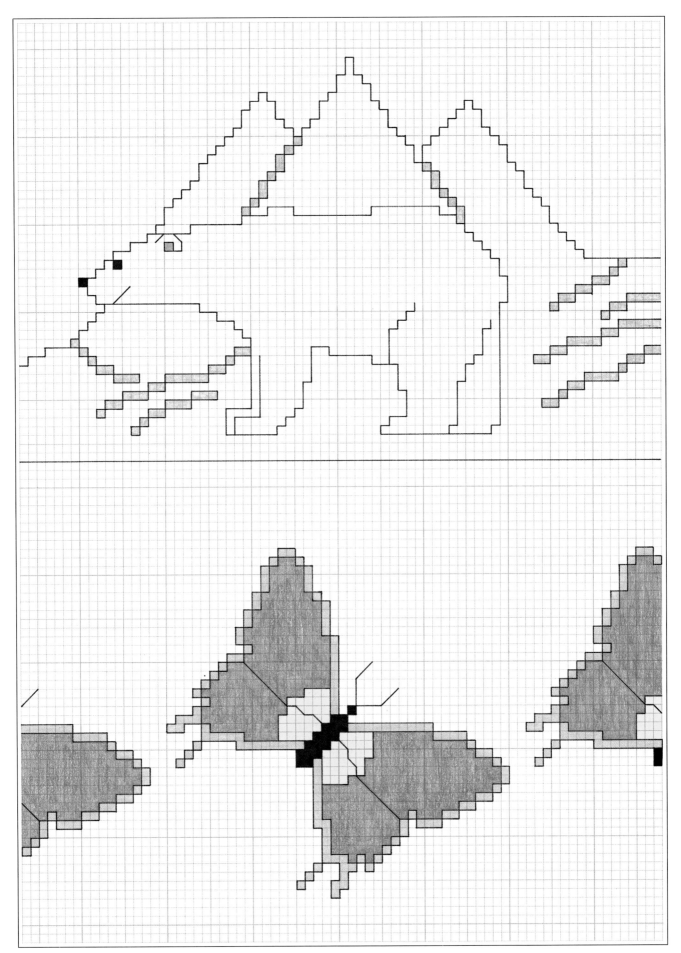

CHART 84 BUTTERFLIES AND BEARS

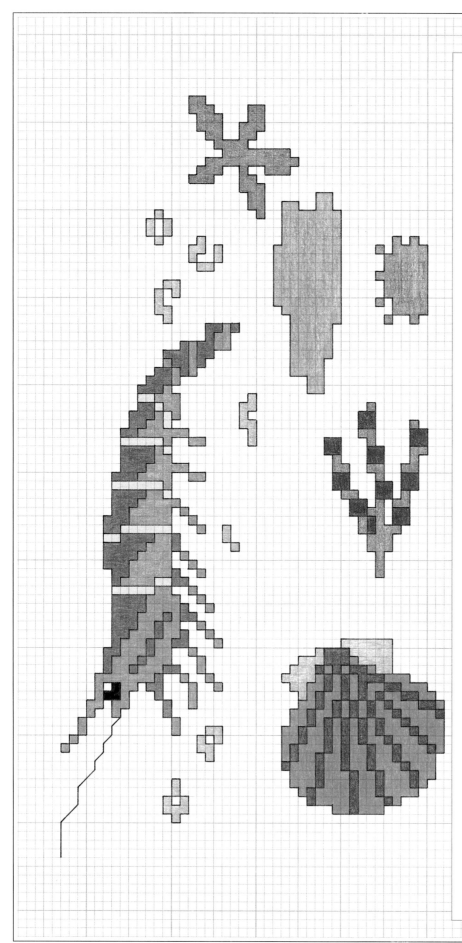

USING THE DESIGNS

Maritime subjects are always in demand – especially for bathrooms, where the designs shown here would be immediately at home. This giant shrimp, with its accompanying starfish, scallop shell and seaweed, would make a most attractive decoration for towels and bathroom curtains (drapes), perhaps even repeated on a towelling bathmat.

Using Waste Canvas
Cross stitch on this type of non-evenweave background is easy if you use waste canvas. Simply tack (baste) a large enough piece of the white canvas to the area you wish to embroider, then work the design over the threads of the canvas.

If you are afraid that your embroidery cotton (floss) will catch and snag against the cut edges of the waste canvas, it is a good idea to bind it with adhesive tape before tacking (basting) it to the fabric. When the embroidery is finished, dampen the canvas thoroughly to soften the glue that holds it together; the threads will then be released and can be carefully withdrawn, one by one.

A good way to do this is to place your embroidery face up on a thick folded towel. Dip a sponge in clean, warm water and squeeze it out, not too hard. Then dab it firmly all over the embroidered canvas, including the outer edges, making the work very damp. Allow a few minutes for the water to soak in and do its work, then very carefully draw out the threads, one at a time, using a pair of tweezers. If the threads don't release easily, make the sponge a little wetter and try again. When all the strands of canvas have been removed, press the work thoroughly.

Waste canvas is 27in (68cm) wide, and comes in mesh sizes 8/9, 10, 12 and 14, giving eight/nine, ten, twelve and fourteen stitches to the inch respectively.

CHART 85 ON THE SEA BED

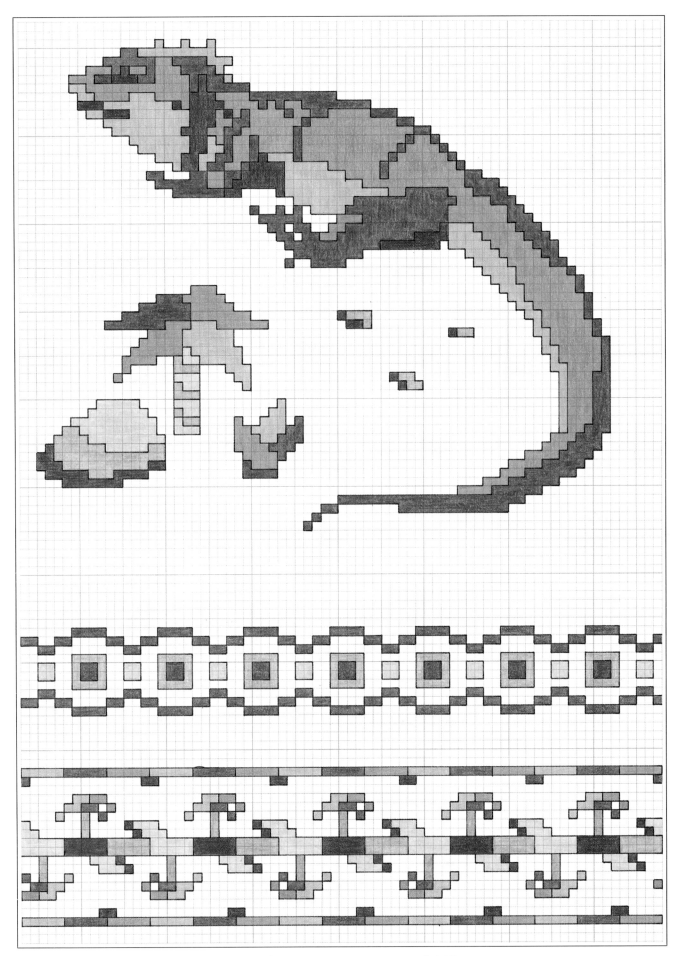

CHART 86 LIZARD AND MATCHING BORDER

USING THE DESIGNS

Fish and other sea creatures seem particularly suitable for cross-stitching, as you can see from the bell pull on page 28.

Making a Bell Pull
If you are not setting your design on an Aida band, choose a suitable background colour in a 14- or 16-count Aida fabric, remembering to allow extra at each side for hems, and at the top and bottom for the channels to hold the hanging devices. The usual method of neatening the edges is to make narrow hems, but this means that your stitches will show on the right side. Instead use Vilene Wundaweb; insert a length of tape under the hem and iron over it with a damp cloth. The hems at the top and bottom can be made in the same way. The finished length of the pull may be anything you wish.

Before you begin, run a tacking (basting) thread directly down the centre of the hanging, from top to bottom. Centre each creature across this line when you stitch, using two strands of embroidery cotton (floss).

The simplest way to hang the bell pull is with two lengths of bamboo which are threaded through the hems at the top and bottom.

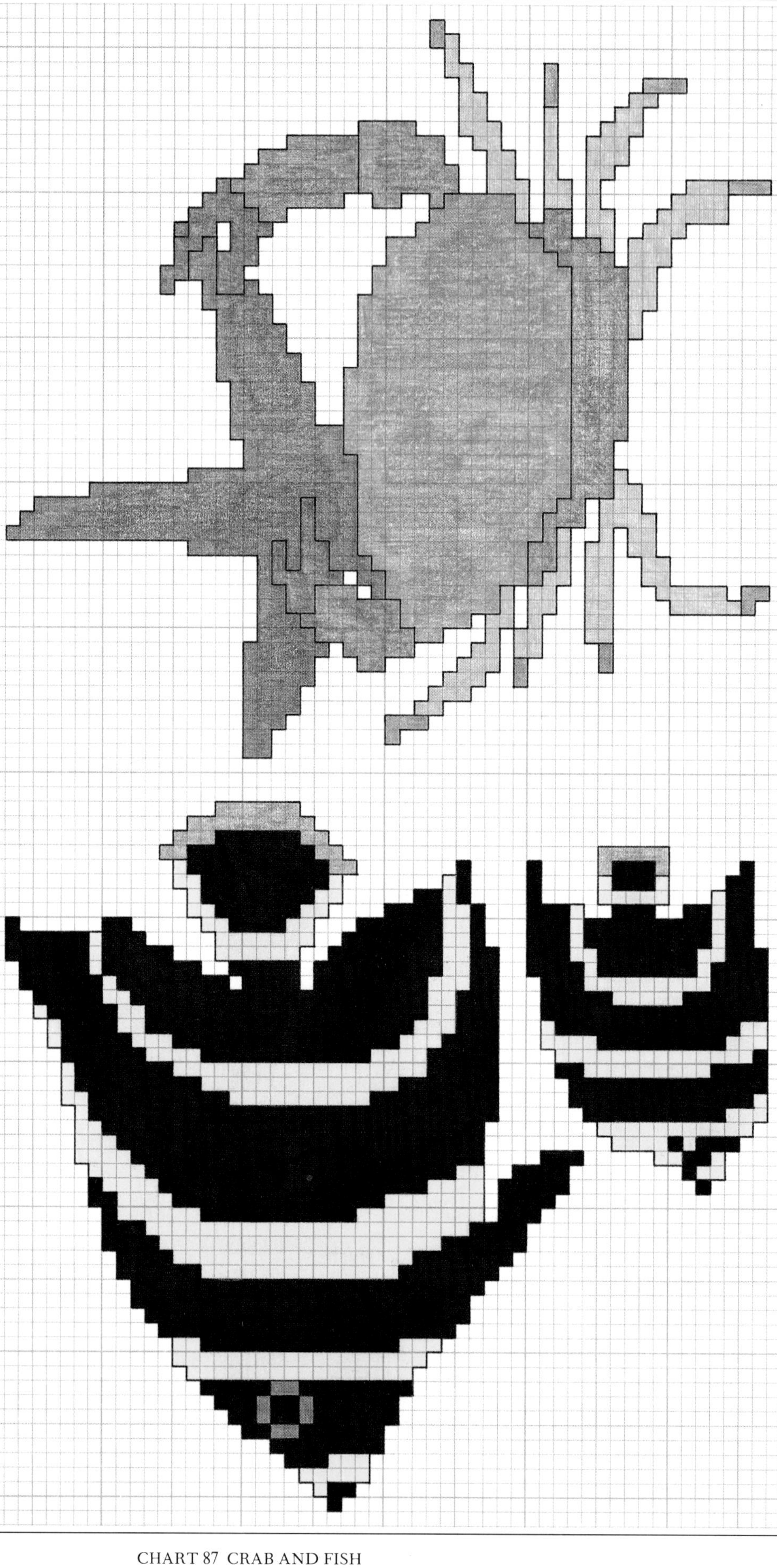

CHART 87 CRAB AND FISH

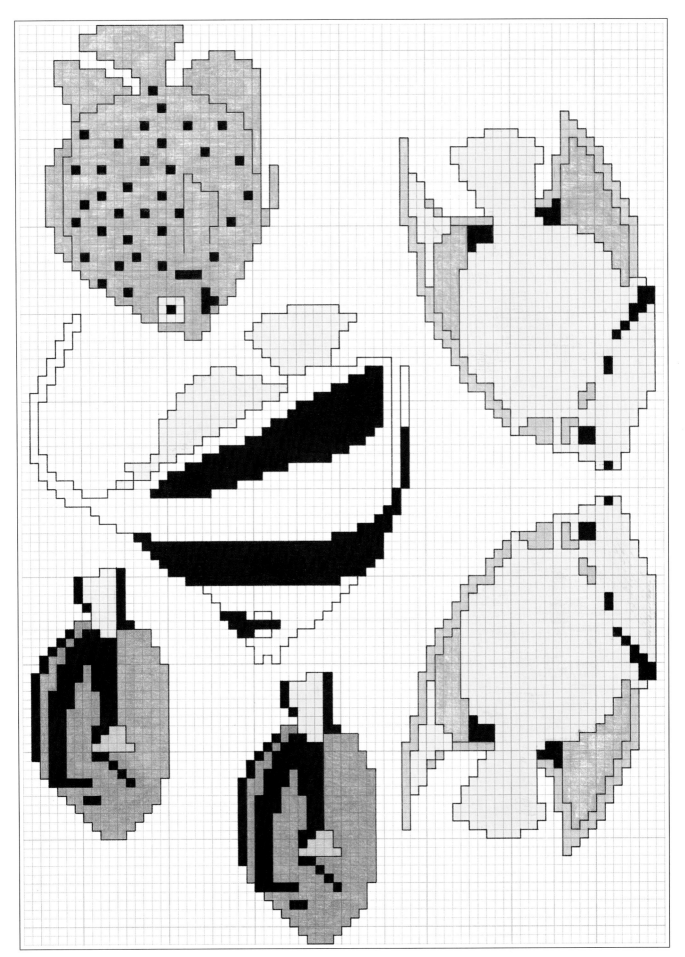

CHART 88 FISHY SUBJECTS

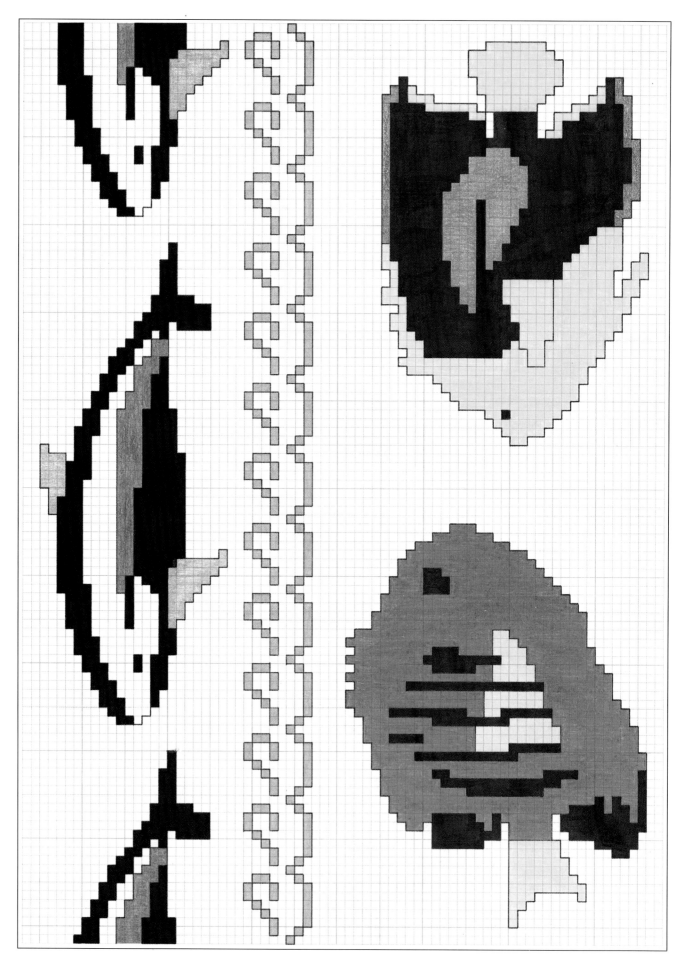

CHART 89 MORE FISHY SUBJECTS

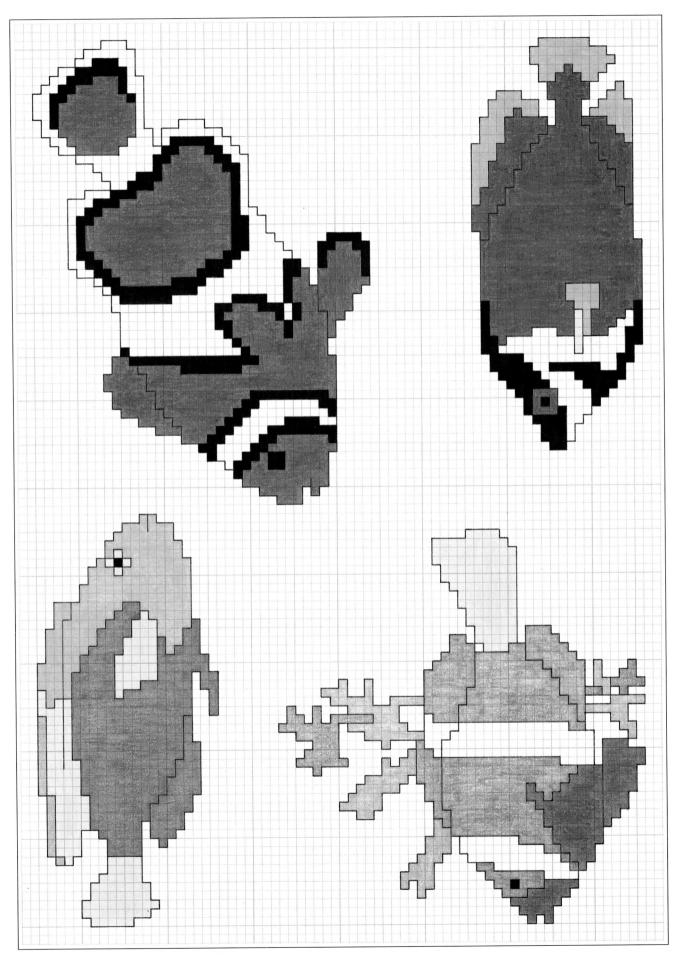

CHART 90 YET MORE FISH

CHART 91 DOWN TO THE SEA AGAIN

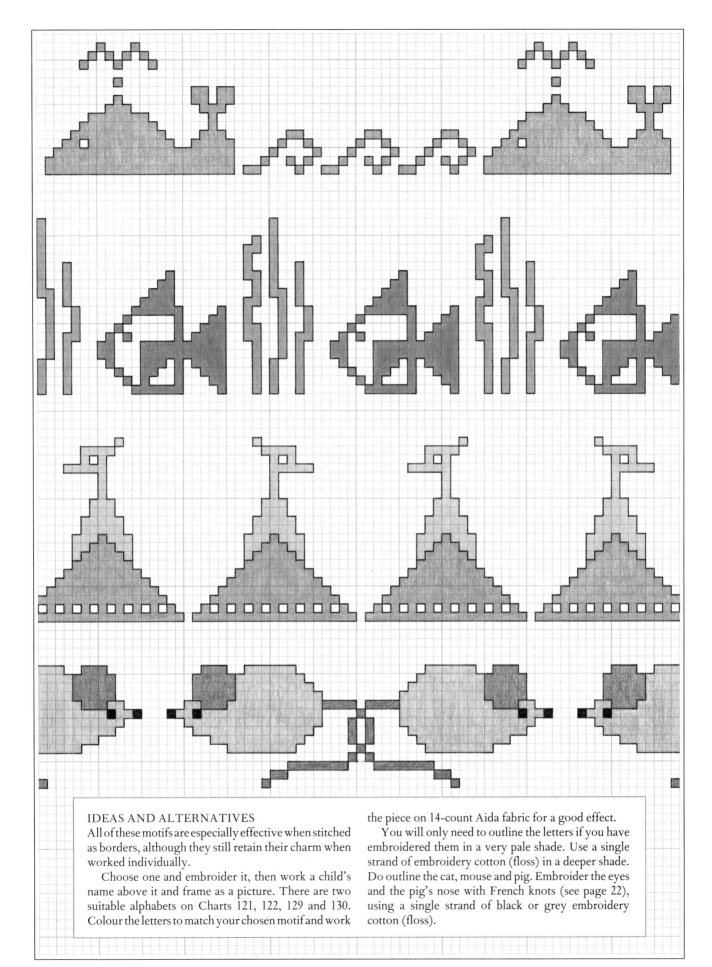

IDEAS AND ALTERNATIVES
All of these motifs are especially effective when stitched as borders, although they still retain their charm when worked individually.

Choose one and embroider it, then work a child's name above it and frame as a picture. There are two suitable alphabets on Charts 121, 122, 129 and 130. Colour the letters to match your chosen motif and work the piece on 14-count Aida fabric for a good effect.

You will only need to outline the letters if you have embroidered them in a very pale shade. Use a single strand of embroidery cotton (floss) in a deeper shade. Do outline the cat, mouse and pig. Embroider the eyes and the pig's nose with French knots (see page 22), using a single strand of black or grey embroidery cotton (floss).

CHART 92 WHALES, FISH, PEACOCKS AND MICE

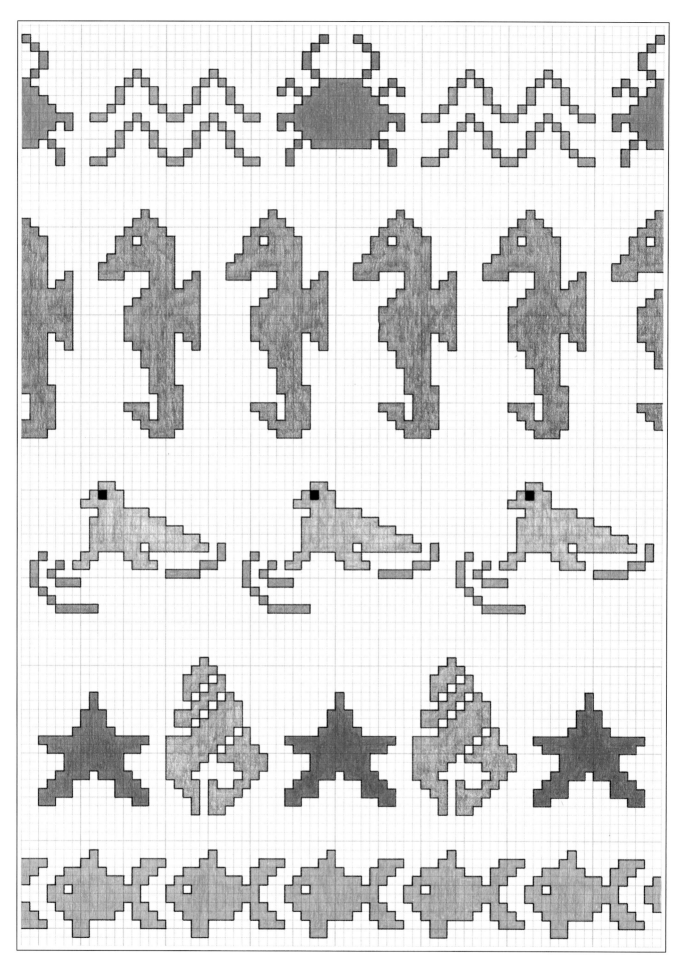

CHART 93 MORE FROM THE SEA

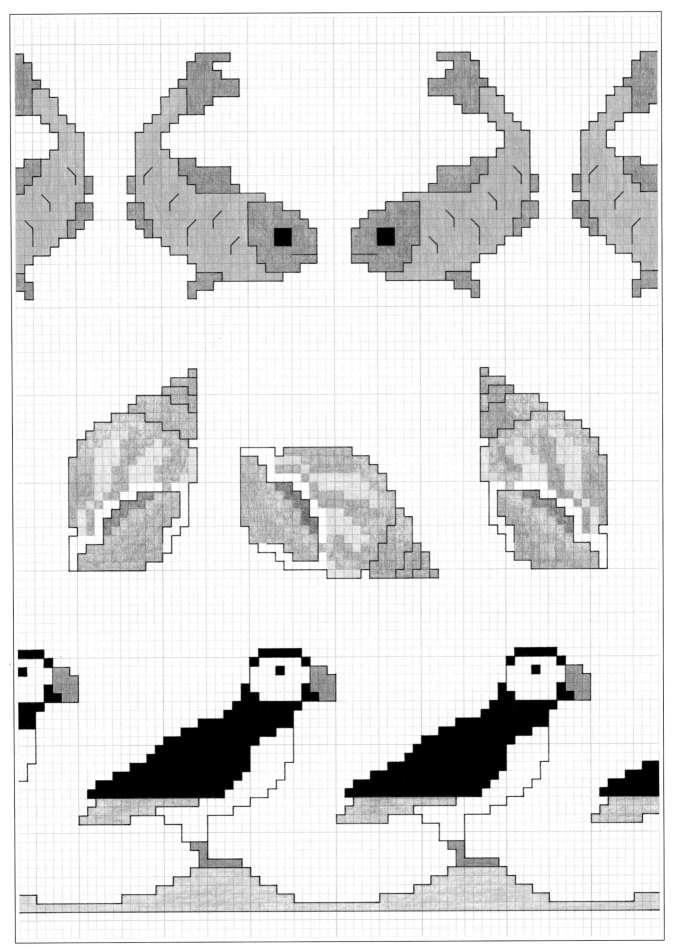

CHART 94 FISH, SHELLS AND PUFFINS

USING THE DESIGN

The mythical unicorn makes a particularly elegant and regal subject for cross stitch, as can be seen in the photograph of the framed picture on page 4. Silvery-white unicorns have been part of history in art and needlework for many centuries. They are still as popular today as they ever were, partly due to their magical associations, but also, no doubt, because they have such a mystical beauty.

The traditional colour scheme depicted here is particularly alluring, but if you wish to change it, experiment with new ideas on paper before you buy your cottons (floss) and begin to embroider.

Copy the design out onto graph paper and colour it in with watercolour paints, crayons or felt-tip pens. The last of these are specially suitable for this purpose,

and inexpensive to buy. Get a large pack, to give yourself a good range of colours from which to choose. Graph paper is widely available; don't go to a specialist art supplier where it will be far more expensive. This is a case when quantity counts far more than quality. Bear in mind that you will want to be able to screw up a sheet and throw it away without feeling that to start again would be wasteful.

Work with a ruler and a fairly soft pencil – HB or B – so that you can rub out easily if you go wrong. When you have drawn out the design and coloured it in, you may wish to go over it with a ballpoint pen to indicate the areas you wish to outline and pick out for emphasis when you have finished your cross stitch. It is very useful to work this out on paper beforehand, as it helps you to visualise the finished work.

CHART 95 UNICORN

IDEAS AND ALTERNATIVES

Horses are such beautifully streamlined creatures and present a challenge to depict in cross stitch. You can see the two lower horses on the greetings card on page 9.

The horses in the top row would make an unusual 14in (35cm) square cushion, if the design was repeated in five horizontal lines, each divided by the triple-square border shown above the trotting horses. The animals would look even more effective if each row was in a different colour.

CHART 96 HORSES FOR COURSES

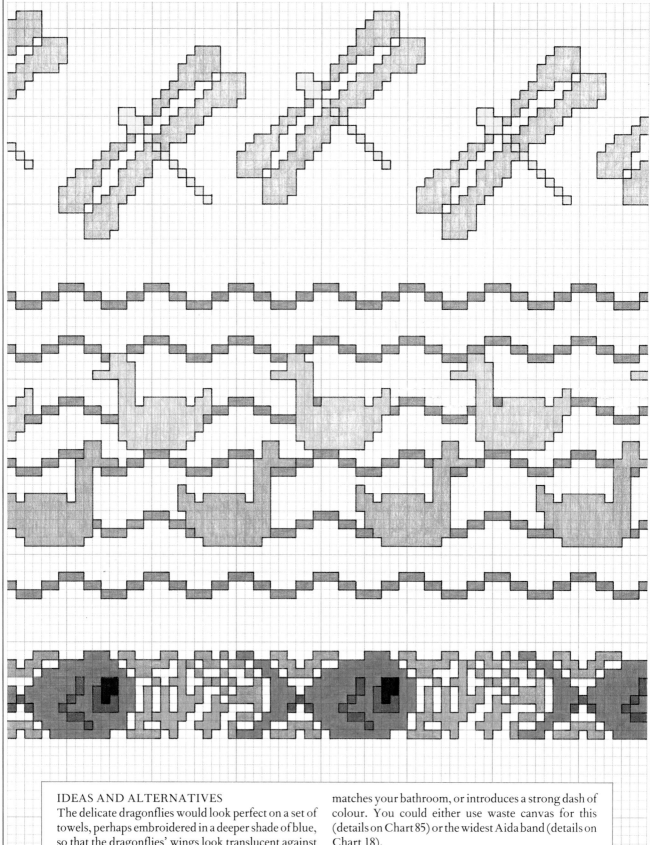

IDEAS AND ALTERNATIVES

The delicate dragonflies would look perfect on a set of towels, perhaps embroidered in a deeper shade of blue, so that the dragonflies' wings look translucent against the darker ground.

The swimming ducks could be repeated at the bottom of a bathroom blind in a colour scheme which matches your bathroom, or introduces a strong dash of colour. You could either use waste canvas for this (details on Chart 85) or the widest Aida band (details on Chart 18).

As for the fish, stitched on a narrow Aida band, they would make a lovely theme to decorate your existing curtains (drapes) and match your towels.

CHART 97 DRAGONFLIES AND DUCKS

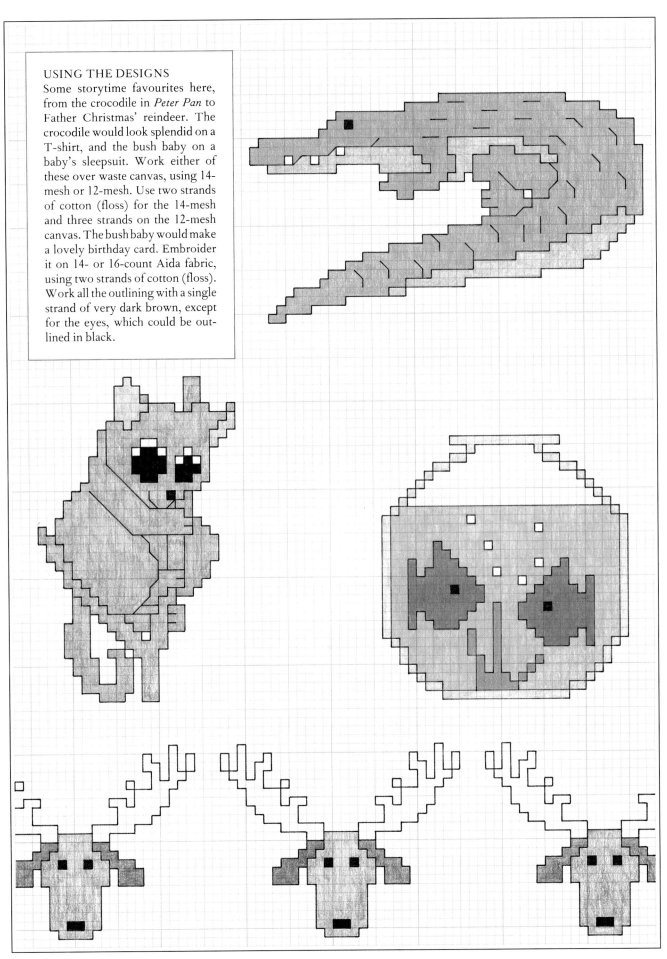

USING THE DESIGNS

Some storytime favourites here, from the crocodile in *Peter Pan* to Father Christmas' reindeer. The crocodile would look splendid on a T-shirt, and the bush baby on a baby's sleepsuit. Work either of these over waste canvas, using 14-mesh or 12-mesh. Use two strands of cotton (floss) for the 14-mesh and three strands on the 12-mesh canvas. The bush baby would make a lovely birthday card. Embroider it on 14- or 16-count Aida fabric, using two strands of cotton (floss). Work all the outlining with a single strand of very dark brown, except for the eyes, which could be outlined in black.

CHART 98 AN ADORABLE ASSORTMENT

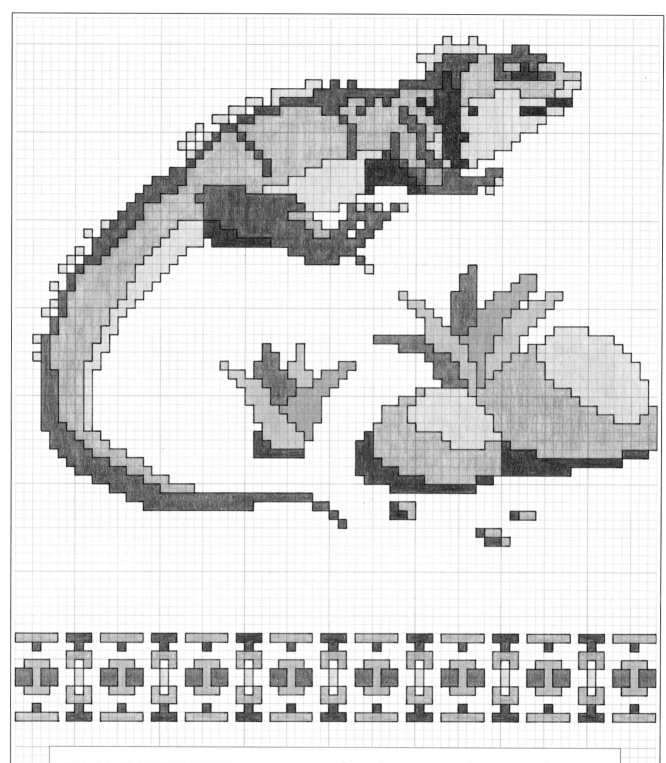

IDEAS AND ALTERNATIVES
Charts 99 and 100 feature subjects with special appeal to boys. If you are planning to embroider the lizard, try to retain the matching border, which incorporates the colours of the lizard and his terrain.

Note the shading of the lizard's skin; this has been deliberately emphasised so that it will be easy for you to follow on the chart. When you choose your embroidery cottons (floss) you can get the two shades of brown, the gold and the yellow a lot closer, so that the

four colours merge much more naturally into one another. But do take care not to go too far in the opposite direction – if you select shades which are too near to one another, you will lose the effect of his realistically variegated skin.

Try to be imaginative with background colours too. Use 14-count Aida and consider the lizard on khaki, sky blue, parchment or sage; and the dinosaur – according to the colours you choose for the creature itself – against Christmas red, navy, green or pewter.

CHART 99 LIZARD

CHART 100 DINOSAUR, SNAKE, GIRAFFE AND OSTRICH

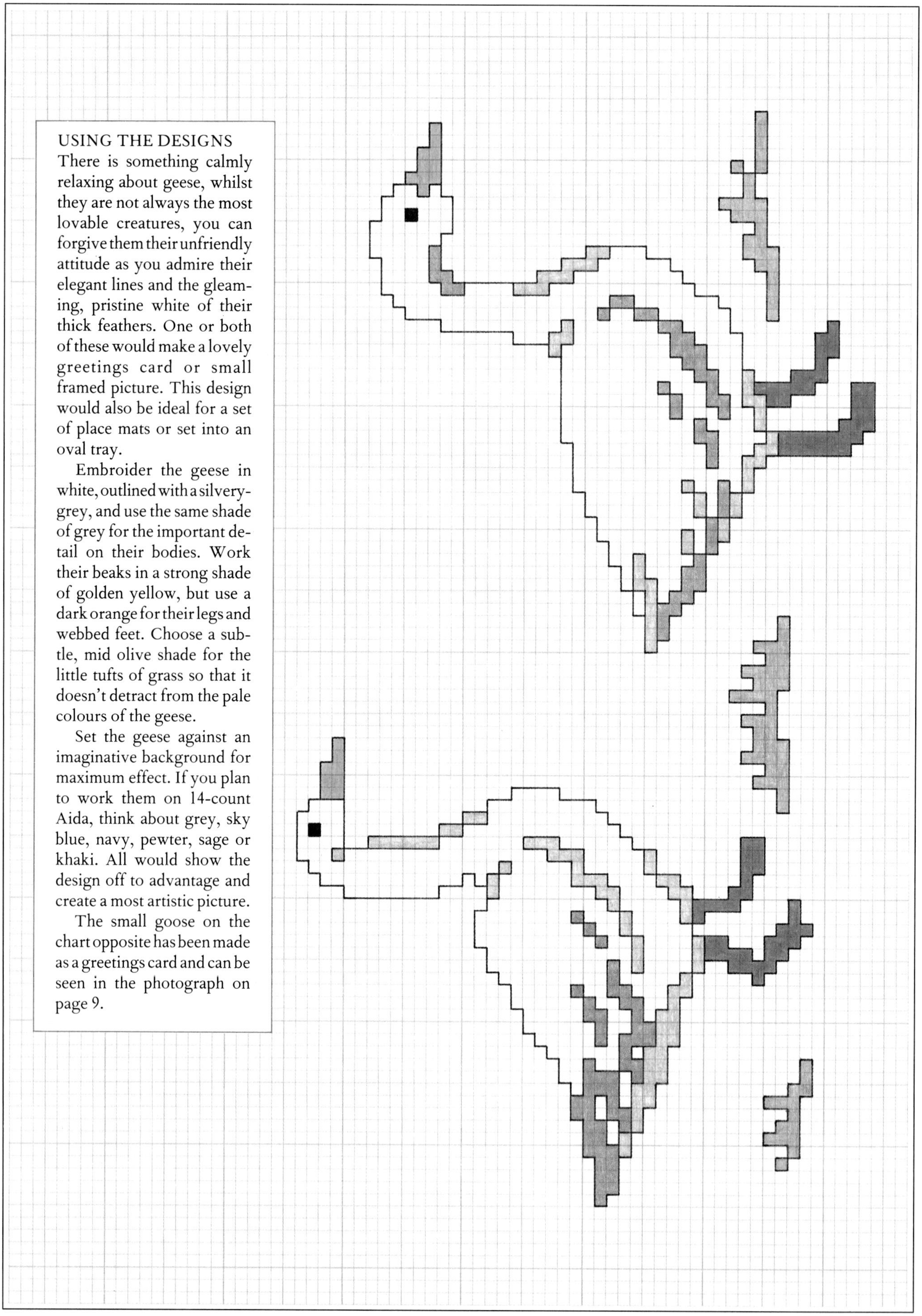

USING THE DESIGNS

There is something calmly relaxing about geese, whilst they are not always the most lovable creatures, you can forgive them their unfriendly attitude as you admire their elegant lines and the gleaming, pristine white of their thick feathers. One or both of these would make a lovely greetings card or small framed picture. This design would also be ideal for a set of place mats or set into an oval tray.

Embroider the geese in white, outlined with a silvery-grey, and use the same shade of grey for the important detail on their bodies. Work their beaks in a strong shade of golden yellow, but use a dark orange for their legs and webbed feet. Choose a subtle, mid olive shade for the little tufts of grass so that it doesn't detract from the pale colours of the geese.

Set the geese against an imaginative background for maximum effect. If you plan to work them on 14-count Aida, think about grey, sky blue, navy, pewter, sage or khaki. All would show the design off to advantage and create a most artistic picture.

The small goose on the chart opposite has been made as a greetings card and can be seen in the photograph on page 9.

CHART 101 ELEGANT GEESE

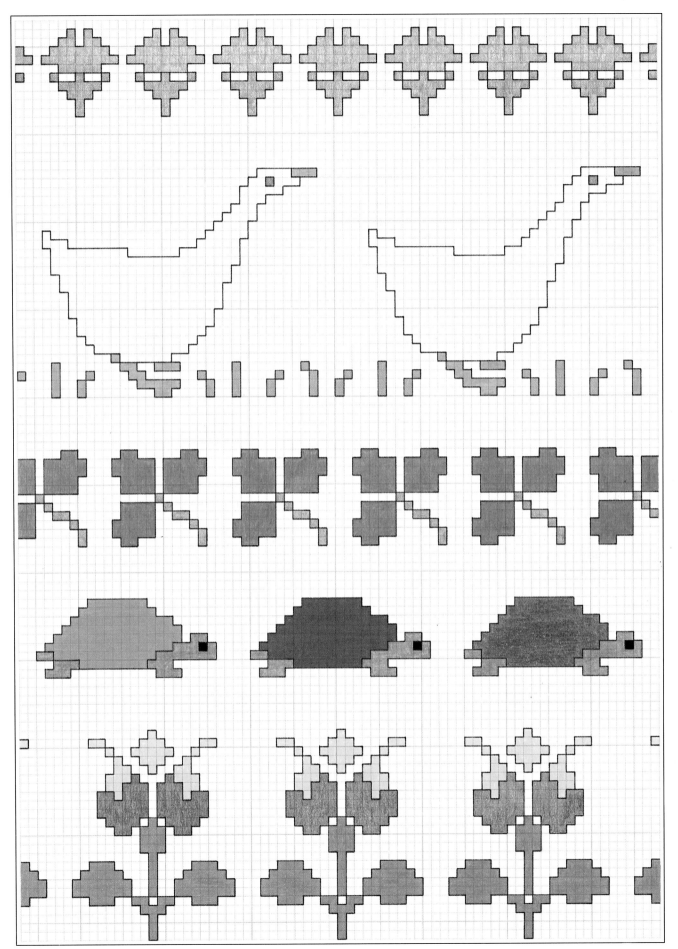

CHART 102 GEESE, TORTOISES, FLOWERS AND LEAVES

CHART 103 CATS AND MORE CATS

CHART 104 DOGS AND MORE DOGS

IDEAS AND ALTERNATIVES

On Charts 105 and 106 there are four very different subjects that would make lovely framed pictures.

The performing seals would be perfect for a child's room. Work them on a strongly coloured background – perhaps Colonial blue or navy Aida, or something bold and bright, like Christmas red or lemon.

The kingfishers are just the reverse. Their colours are so vivid that they need a more subdued background. Sky blue would be the most obvious, but consider khaki, sage, grey, peach or pink. This is another example of subtle shading, where you need to select your embroidery cottons (floss) with great care.

Shading is also important in the lion (Chart 106), the three shades of gold are extremely effective when chosen to create a subtle effect, without becoming indistinguishable.

The ram and the lion would make ideal gifts, mounted in a gilded, circular frame. Both would stand out well against dramatically dark fabrics: for example, grey, holly green, navy, pewter, sage or black.

When choosing the background fabric for any picture, try to take into account the colour and pattern, if any, of the walls on which the pictures are to be hung: especially if you are planning something particularly striking or dramatic.

CHART 105 PERFORMING SEALS

CHART 106 KINGFISHER, RAM AND LION

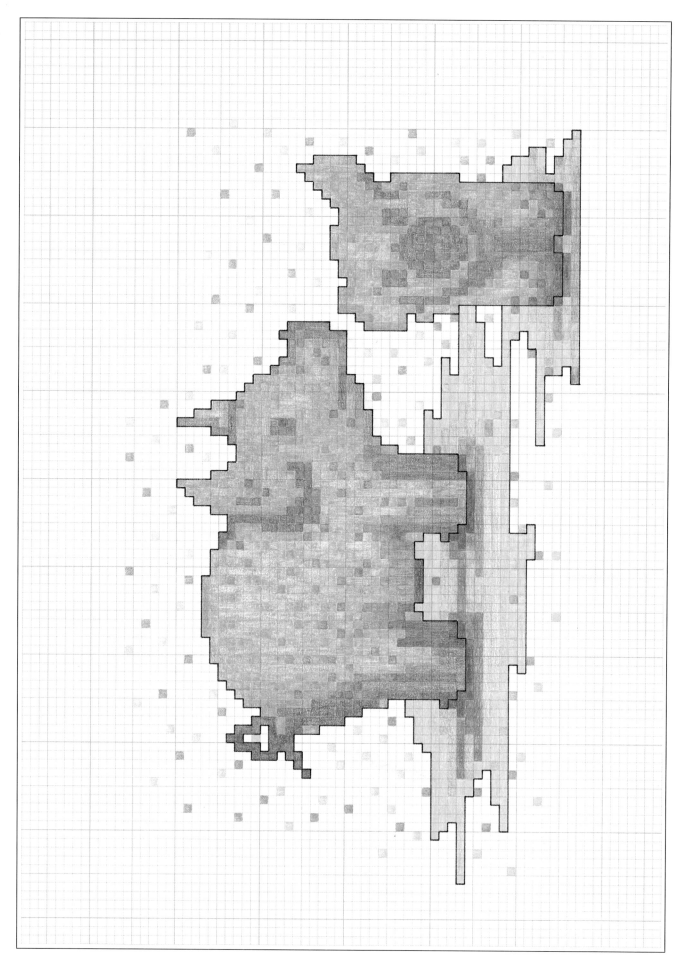

CHART 107 TWO PLUMP PIGS

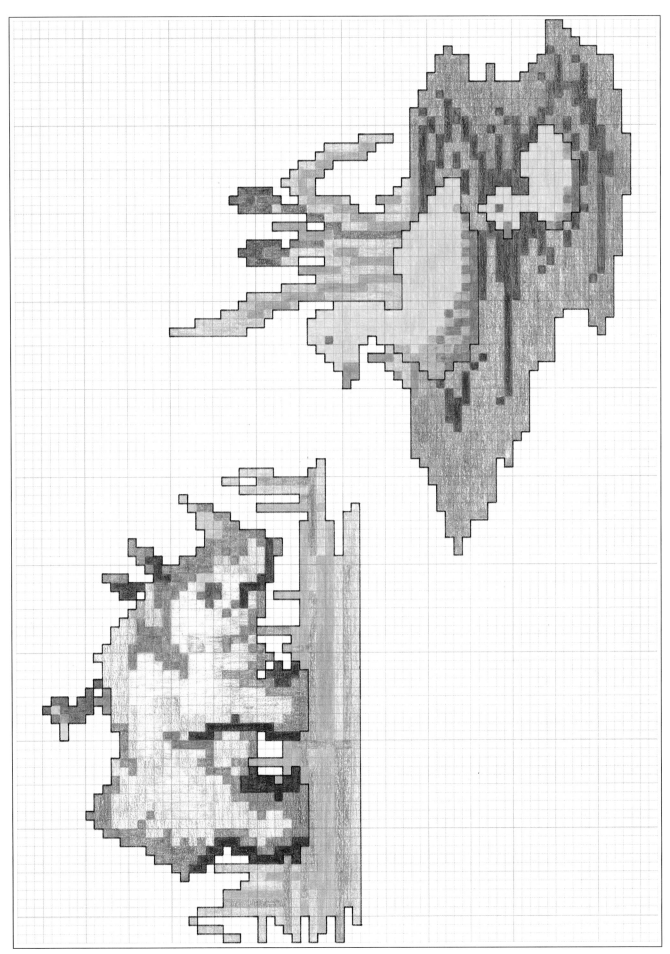

CHART 108 RHINO, DUCK AND DUCKLING

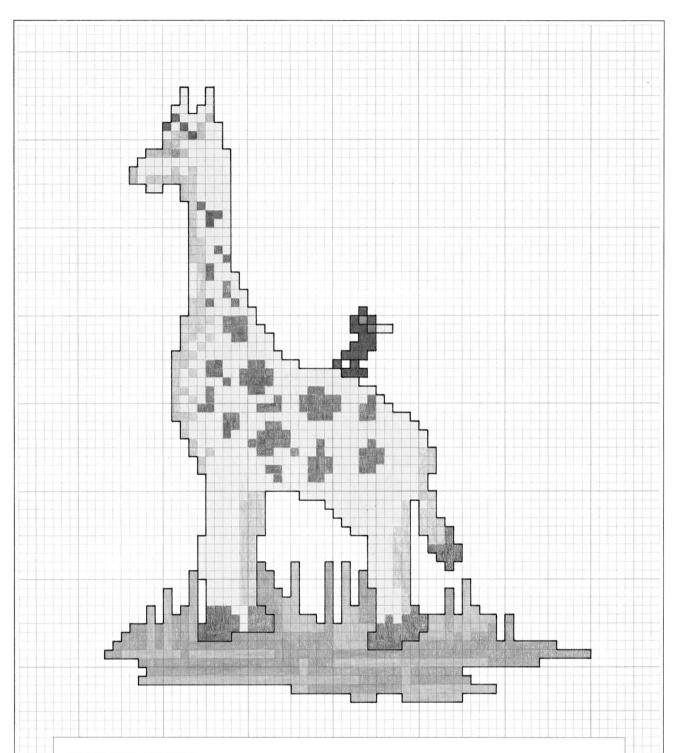

USING THE DESIGNS

Charts 109 and 110 feature two enchanting nursery designs. Work on 14-count Aida fabric on a cream, ecru, sky blue or peach background, using two strands of embroidery cotton (floss). When framing choose a colourful mount for each subject, e.g. deep gold for the giraffe and pink for the monkeys.

Mounting a Picture
You can frame your work yourself by just making a simple mount from either coloured cartridge paper or fabric (cotton poplin is a good choice).

You can buy cartridge paper from artists' supply shops, which offer a good selection, but choose your colour carefully. Take a piece of the background fabric with you, together with all the embroidery cottons (floss) you used. Or take the embroidery itself, so that you can judge how each colour looks against the papers on offer. Avoid having the paper rolled if possible. Carry it flat, either in a portfolio or between two sheets of card. Rolling can produce blemishes or little wrinkles, but if this happens, try smoothing the paper with a warm iron.   ▷

CHART 109 NURSERY PICTURE

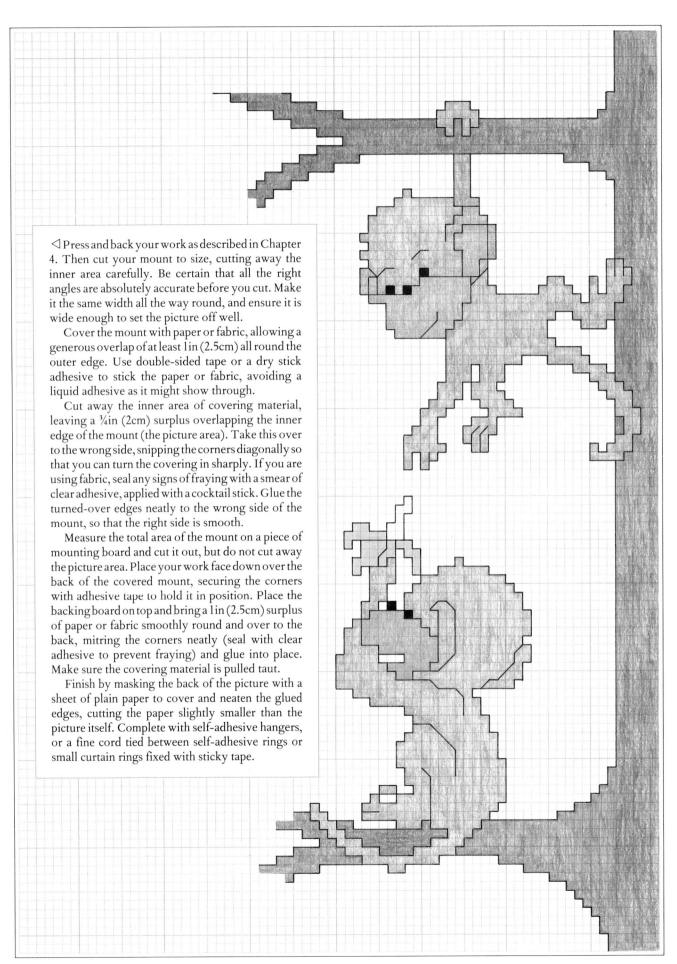

◁ Press and back your work as described in Chapter 4. Then cut your mount to size, cutting away the inner area carefully. Be certain that all the right angles are absolutely accurate before you cut. Make it the same width all the way round, and ensure it is wide enough to set the picture off well.

Cover the mount with paper or fabric, allowing a generous overlap of at least 1in (2.5cm) all round the outer edge. Use double-sided tape or a dry stick adhesive to stick the paper or fabric, avoiding a liquid adhesive as it might show through.

Cut away the inner area of covering material, leaving a ¾in (2cm) surplus overlapping the inner edge of the mount (the picture area). Take this over to the wrong side, snipping the corners diagonally so that you can turn the covering in sharply. If you are using fabric, seal any signs of fraying with a smear of clear adhesive, applied with a cocktail stick. Glue the turned-over edges neatly to the wrong side of the mount, so that the right side is smooth.

Measure the total area of the mount on a piece of mounting board and cut it out, but do not cut away the picture area. Place your work face down over the back of the covered mount, securing the corners with adhesive tape to hold it in position. Place the backing board on top and bring a 1in (2.5cm) surplus of paper or fabric smoothly round and over to the back, mitring the corners neatly (seal with clear adhesive to prevent fraying) and glue into place. Make sure the covering material is pulled taut.

Finish by masking the back of the picture with a sheet of plain paper to cover and neaten the glued edges, cutting the paper slightly smaller than the picture itself. Complete with self-adhesive hangers, or a fine cord tied between self-adhesive rings or small curtain rings fixed with sticky tape.

CHART 110 NURSERY PICTURE 2

CHART 111 ELEPHANTS AND BALLOONS

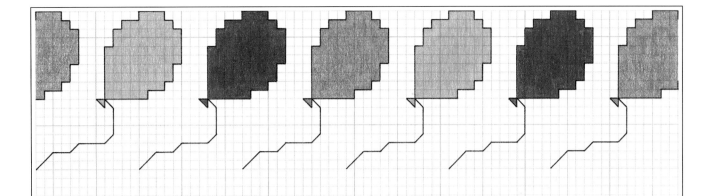

IDEAS AND ALTERNATIVES

This design makes an enchanting picture (see the photograph on page 2) but it would also make an unusual border decoration for a pair of curtains (drapes). Reverse the design so that two mother elephants meet at the centre, with their respective families behind them. A pair of Aida bands embroidered with a line of balloons would make matching tie-backs.

The design would also be perfect for a child's place mat, the elephants along the base and balloons along the top. A matching bib could have some baby elephants trotting across it.

If you do not want to make up your own place mats, you can buy them ready-prepared, with a fringed edge. Measuring 19 × 13 in (48 × 33cm), they come in white or cream 26-count evenweave fabric, which means you can embroider over two threads in each direction, giving thirteen stitches to the inch. Work the cross stitches with two strands of embroidery cotton (floss), and outline with a single one.

For a picture, use 14- or 16-count Aida, with two strands of embroidery cotton (floss). For curtains (drapes), use waste canvas on plain fabric. Outline the elephants with a single strand of cotton (floss) in a darker grey, and embroider the leg detail with a single strand of black.

The design could also make a cover for a child's cot, with the elephants at the bottom and balloons along the top.

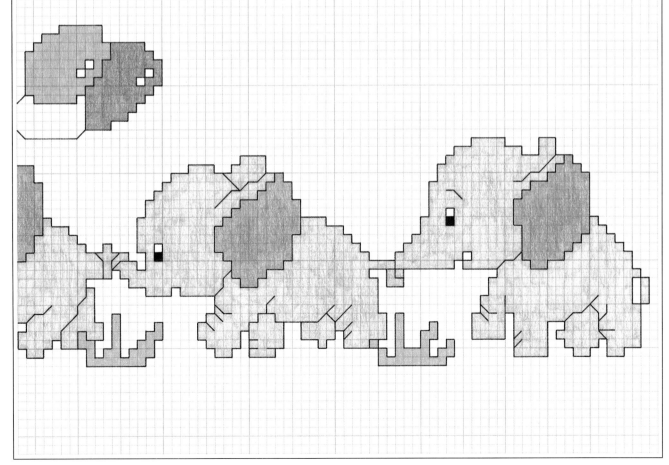

CHART 112 ELEPHANT AND BALLOONS continued

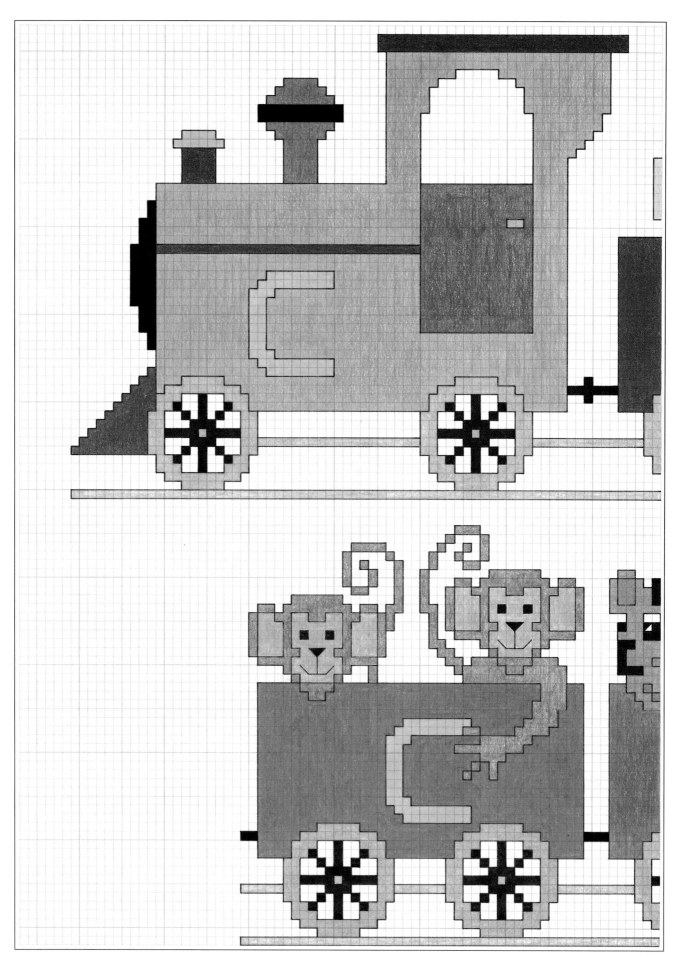

CHART 113 CIRCUS TRAIN

CHART 114 CIRCUS TRAIN continued

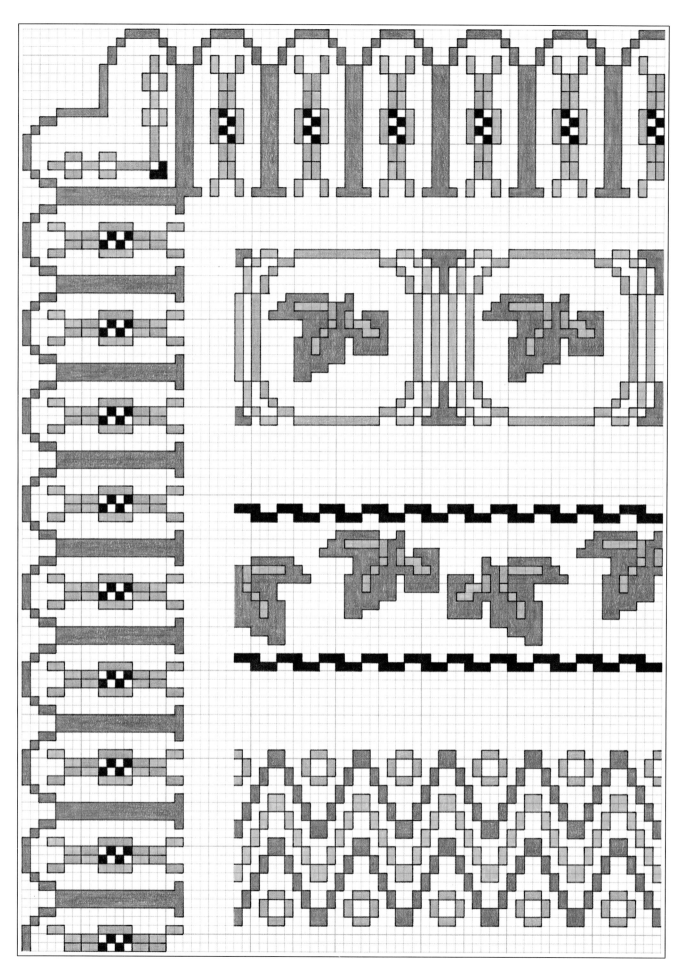

CHART 115 BOLD BORDERS

CHART 116 FOLK ART BORDERS

IDEAS AND ALTERNATIVES

These floral borders are particularly suitable for kitchens, but they could be adapted for many purposes.

One attractive suggestion is to make them into a door finger-plate. The embroidery is easily mounted behind the finger-plate, which is then screwed into position on the door. In each case, work out the area to be covered, and begin your embroidery in the centre, as described in Chapter 3. Many other designs in this book would also make attractive finger plates.

CHART 117 KITCHEN FLORALS

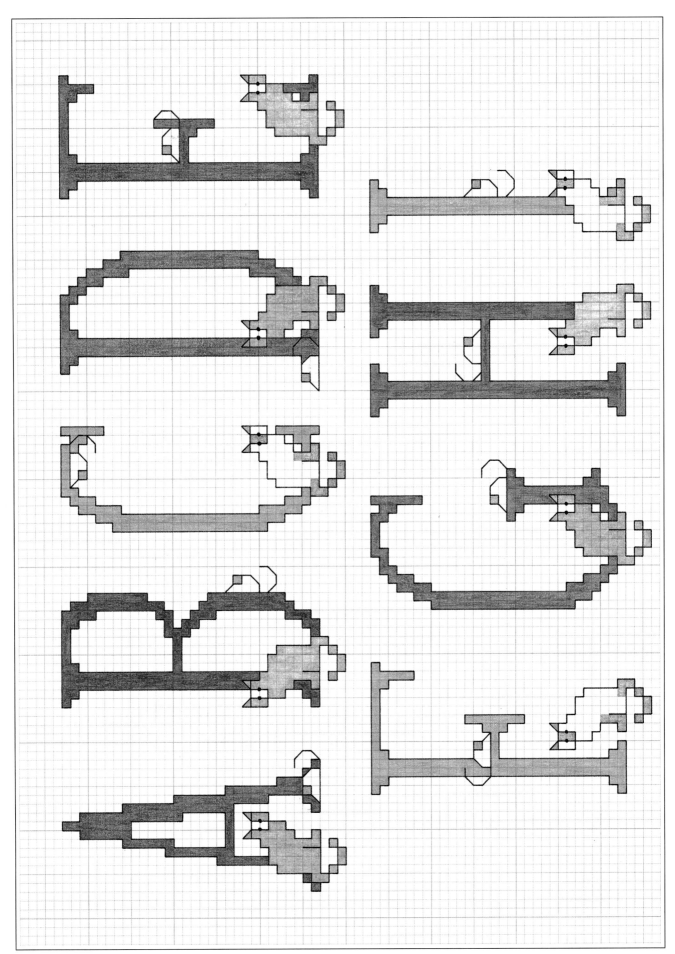

CHART 118 CAT AND MOUSE ALPHABET

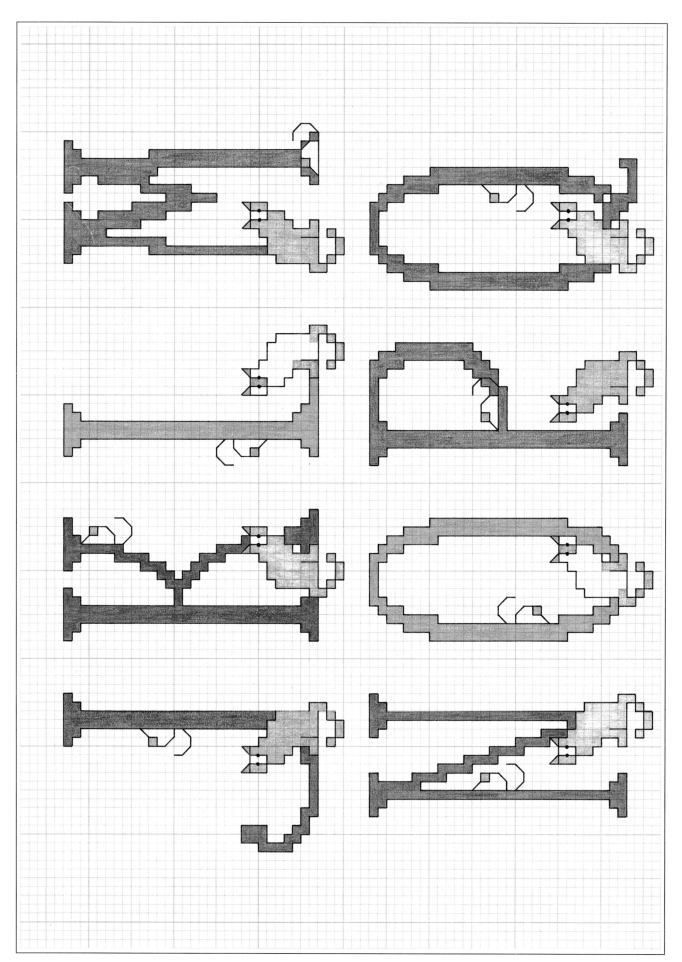

CHART 119 CAT AND MOUSE ALPHABET continued

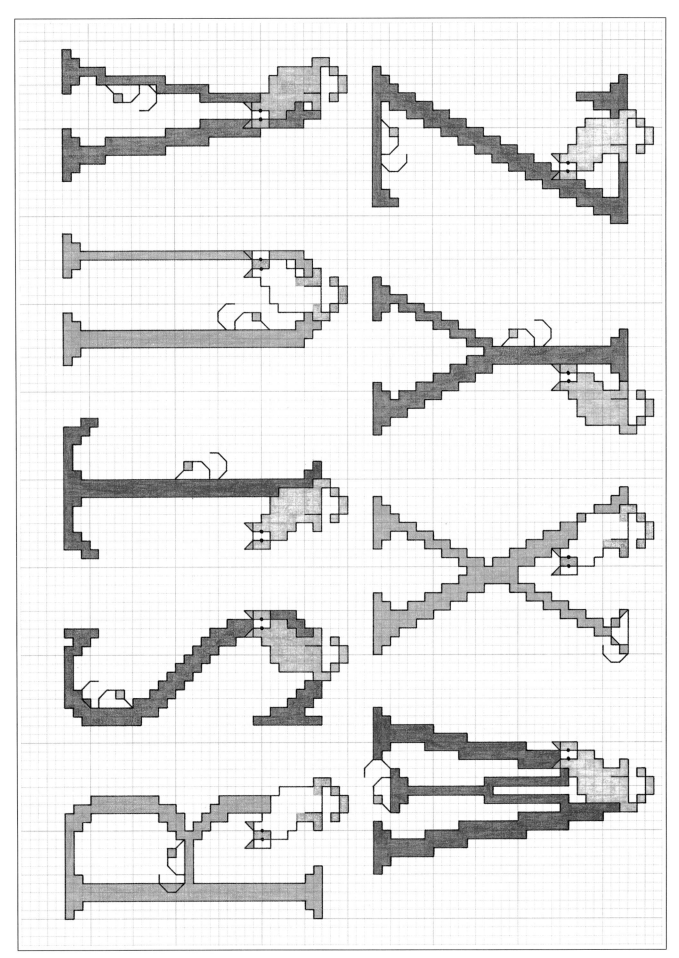

CHART 120 CAT AND MOUSE ALPHABET continued

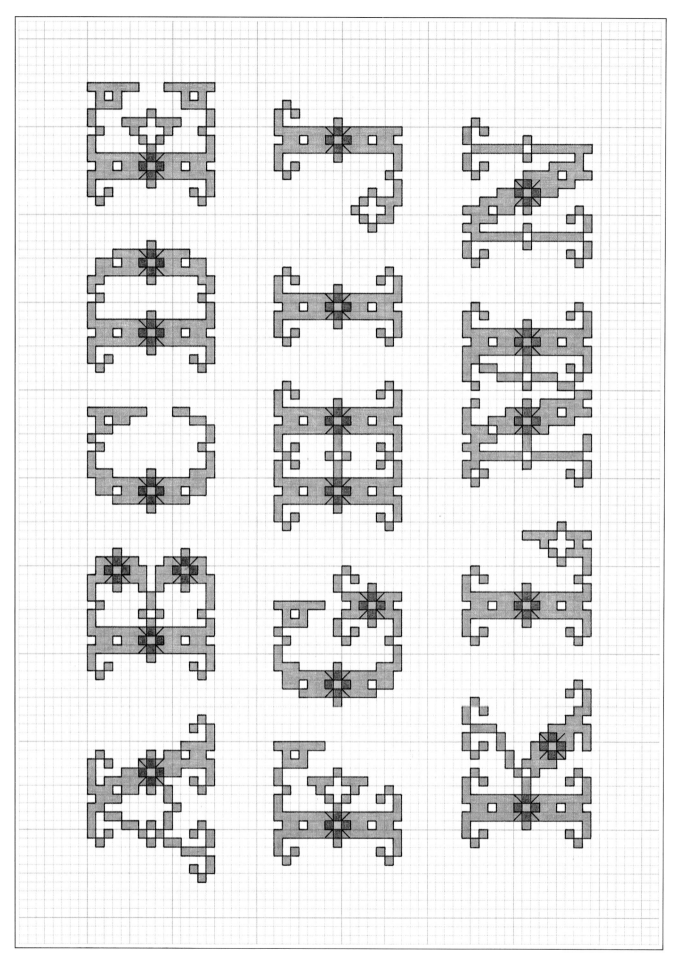

CHART 121 TINY FLOWERS ALPHABET

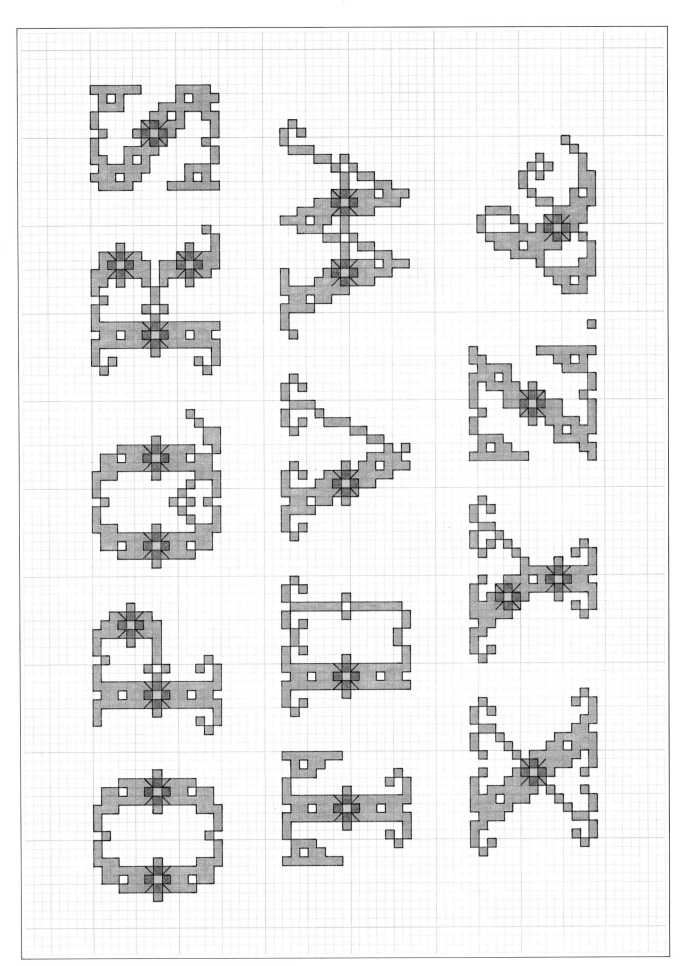

CHART 122 TINY FLOWERS ALPHABET continued

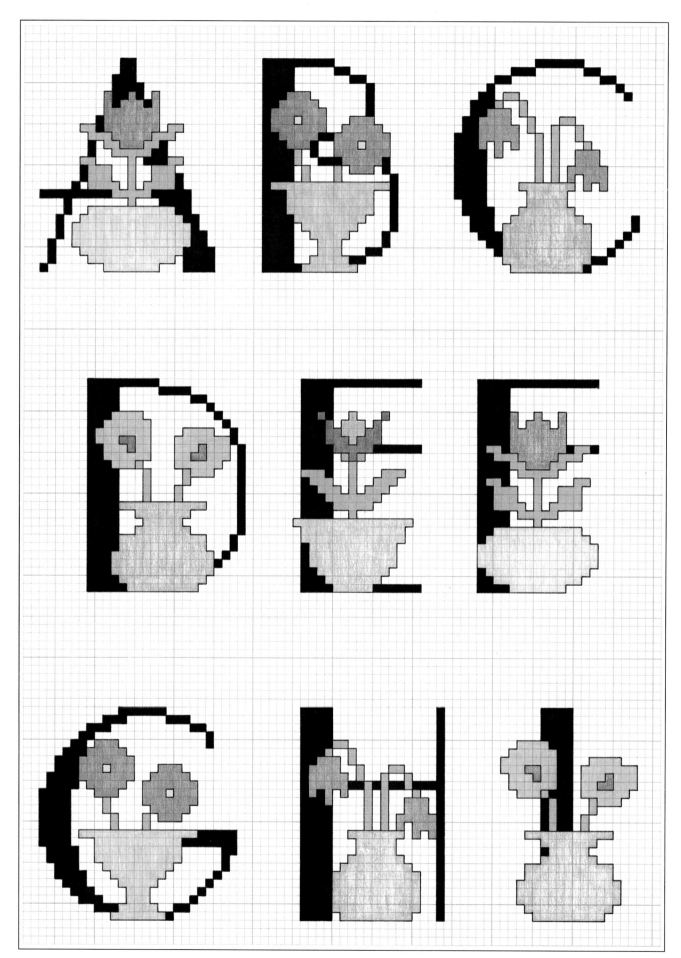

CHART 123 VASES OF FLOWERS ALPHABET

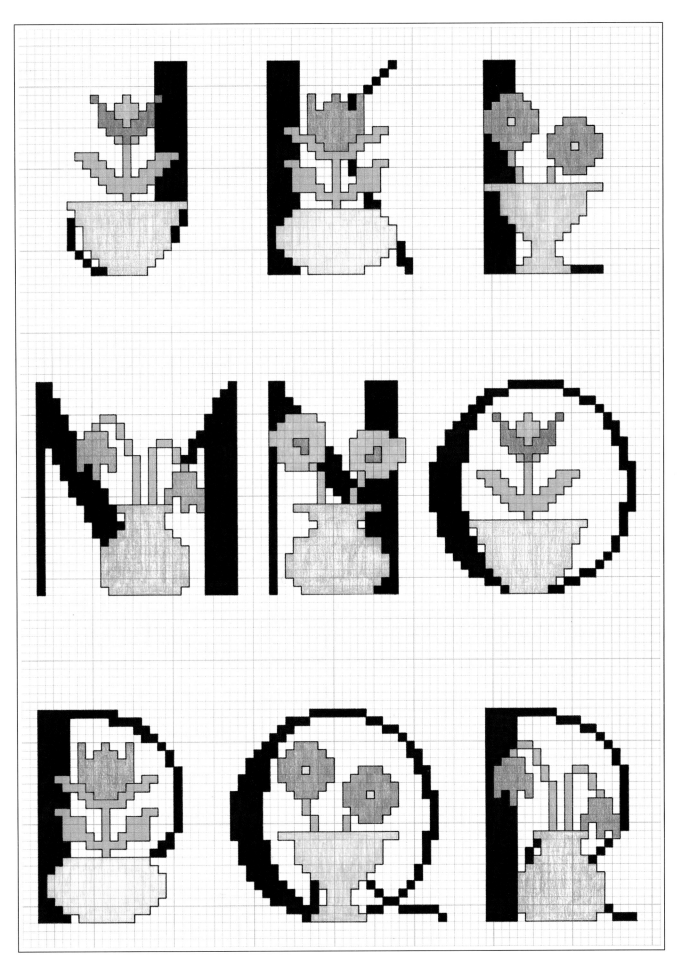

CHART 124 VASES OF FLOWERS ALPHABET continued

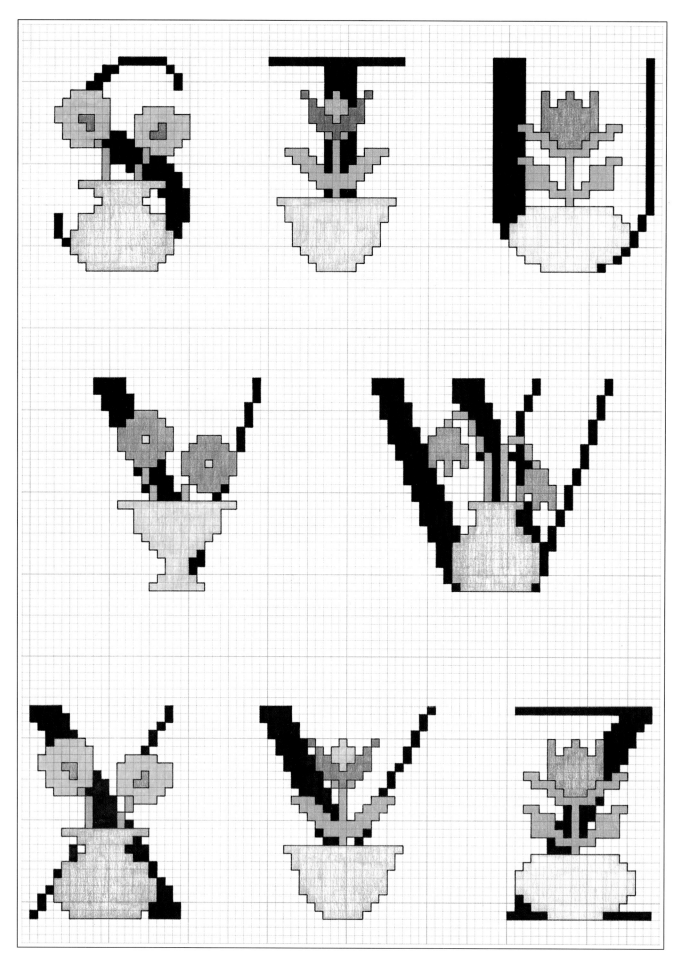

CHART 125 VASES OF FLOWERS ALPHABET continued

CHART 126 PIGLET ALPHABET

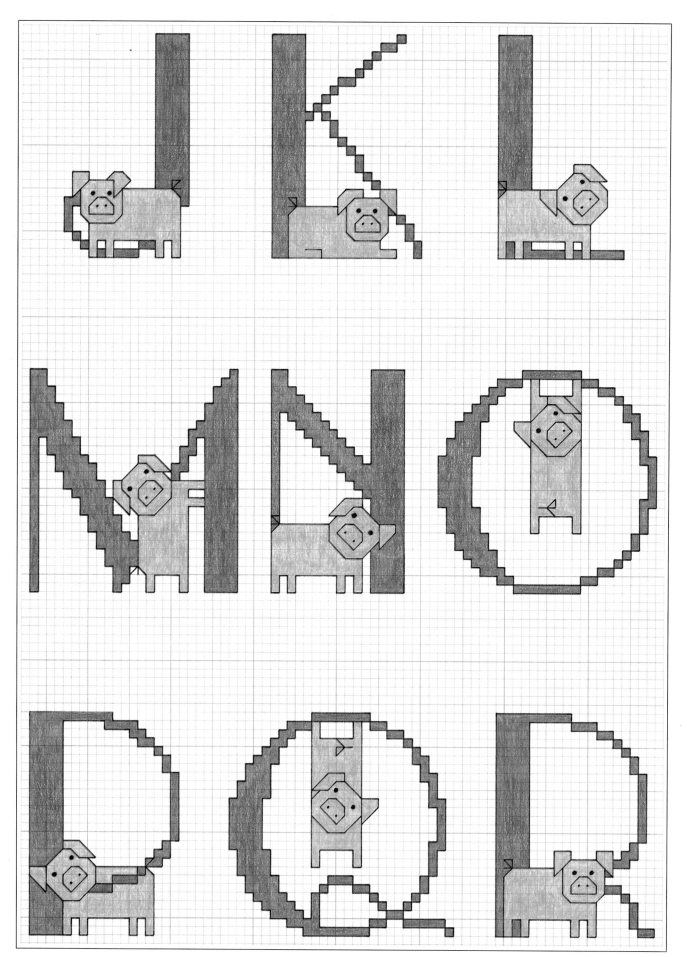

CHART 127 PIGLET ALPHABET continued

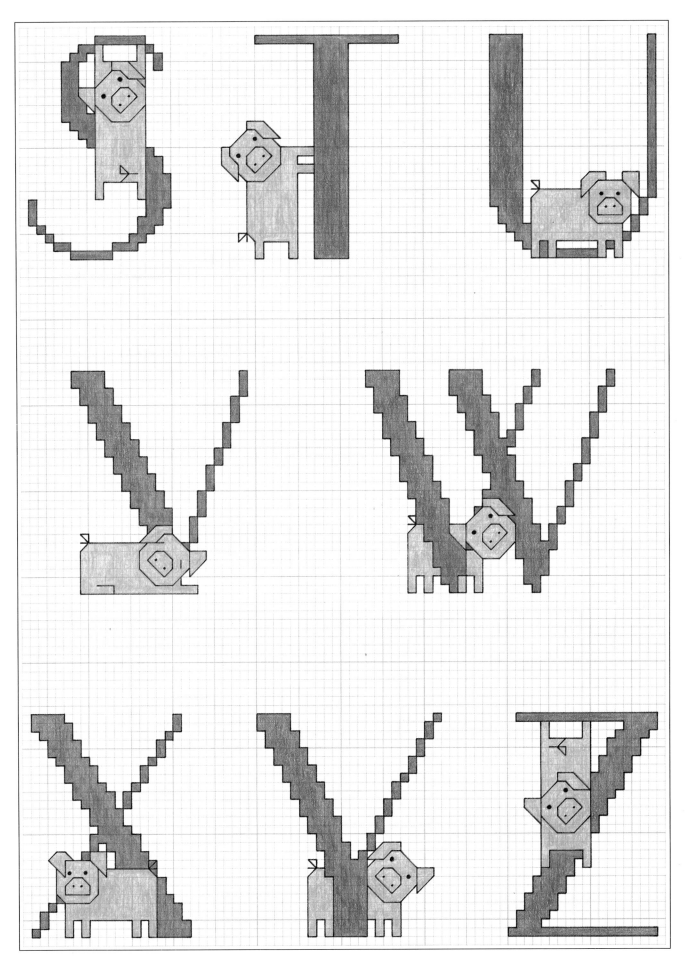

CHART 128 PIGLET ALPHABET continued

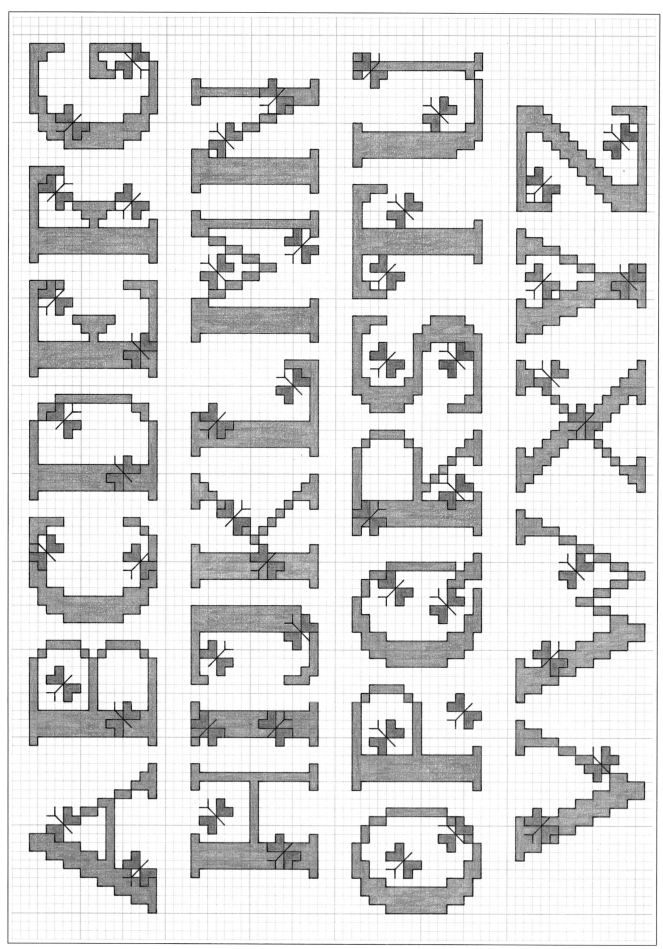

CHART 129 BUTTERFLIES ALPHABET

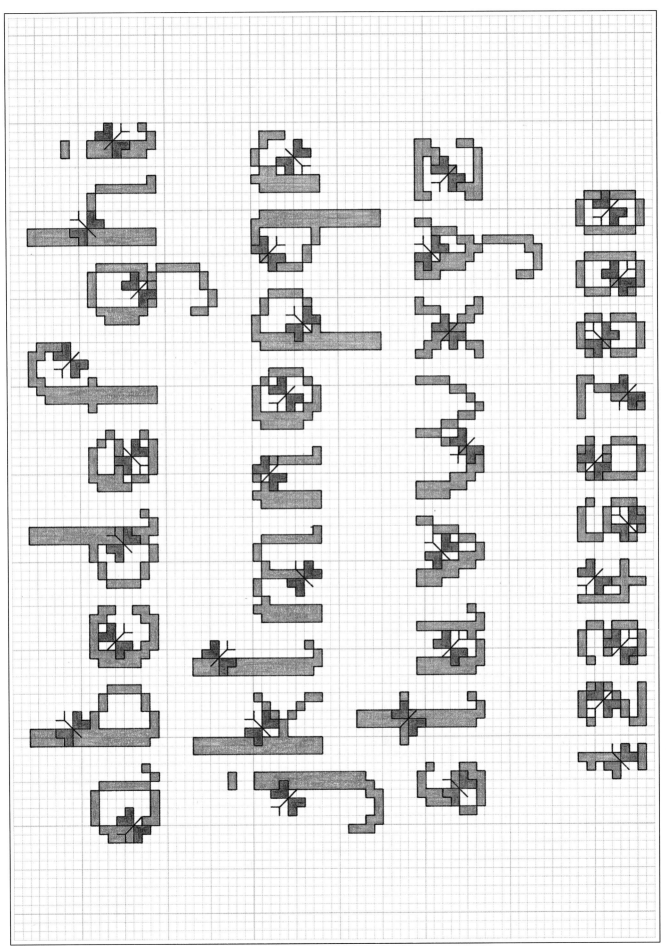

CHART 130 BUTTERFLIES ALPHABET continued

INDEX OF CHARTS AND PROJECTS

The numbers beside each subject indicate charts on which such a design or description of a suggested project, appears.